BFI Film Classics

The BFI Film Classics series introduces, interprets and celebrates landmarks of world cinema. Each volume offers an argument for the film's 'classic' status, together with discussion of its production and reception history, its place within a genre or national cinema, an account of its technical and aesthetic importance, and in many cases, the author's personal response to the film.

For a full list of titles in the series, please visit
https://www.bloomsbury.com/uk/series/bfi-film-classics/

Hanyŏ
[The Housemaid]

Youngmin Choe

THE BRITISH FILM INSTITUTE
Bloomsbury Publishing Plc, 50 Bedford Square, London, WC1B 3DP, UK
Bloomsbury Publishing Inc, 1385 Broadway, New York, NY 10018, USA
Bloomsbury Publishing Ireland, 29 Earlsfort Terrace, Dublin 2, D02 AY28, Ireland

BLOOMSBURY is a trademark of Bloomsbury Publishing Plc

First published in Great Britain 2025 by Bloomsbury on behalf of the
British Film Institute, 21 Stephen Street, London, W1T 1LN
www.bfi.org.uk

The BFI is a cultural charity, a National Lottery distributor, and the UK's lead organisation for film
and the moving image. We believe society needs stories. Film, television and the moving image
bring them to life, helping us to connect and understand each other better. We share the stories
of yesterday, search for the stories of today, and shape the stories of tomorrow.

Cover artwork: © Hokyoung Kim
Series cover design: Louise Dugdale
Series text design: Ketchup/SE14
Images from *Hanyŏ* (Kim Ki-young, 1960), Korean Literature Film Co., Ltd/Kim Ki-young
Productions

A catalogue record for this book is available from the British Library.

Library of Congress Control Number: 2024052529

ISBN: PB: 978-1-8390-2586-0
         ePDF: 978-1-8390-2588-4
         ePUB: 978-1-8390-2587-7

Printed and bound in India

For product safety related questions contact productsafety@bloomsbury.com.

To find out more about our authors and books visit www.bloomsbury.com
and sign up for our newsletters.

Contents

Acknowledgments

Kim Ki-young's *Hanyŏ* has generated a remarkable amount of film criticism and academic research, especially since its rediscovery in the late 1990s. Like the film, television and media homages that credit Kim Ki-young and *Hanyŏ* specifically as a major influence on their own uniquely creative works, the film scholarship that it continues to inspire speaks volumes about *Hanyŏ*'s generative power. In this short book, I have been unable to include all the marvellous work on *Hanyŏ* but I would like to acknowledge how formative they have been in stimulating my own reading. Many thanks to Chris Berry and Soyoung Kim, who first shared with me their deep appreciation for *Hanyŏ* and the works of Kim Ki-young. Funding from the USC Dana and David Dornsife College of Letters, Arts and Sciences; the USC Korean Studies Institute; and the Laboratory Program for Korean Studies and Korean Studies Promotion Service of the Academy of Korean Studies (AKS-2015–LAB-2250002) supported in part the research for this book. Kim Ki-young's son, Kim Dong-yang, generously provided photos of the director and granted permission to use them in this book. Jaeyeong Shin at the Korean Film Archive provided archival images and advised me on copyright matters, and Bellina Jung at the Busan International Film Festival kindly provided the image of Kim Ki-young at the 1997 BIFF. Special thanks to Jinsoo An, Michael Berry, Hye Seung Chung, Kyung Hyun Kim, Akira Lippit and Michael Szalay, and especially to Rebecca Barden, Barbara Cohen Bastos, Anna Coatman and Sophie Contento at Bloomsbury. Most of all, I thank my family and Isobel Jeon, for their interest in every aspect of this book, and Joseph Jeon, for his incisive feedback and boundless support. This book is dedicated to him.

Introduction: *Hanyŏ* and Compressed Modernisation

The film critic Yi Yŏn-ho[1] famously remarked that 'there is a "before" and "after" *Hanyŏ* in Korean film history'.[2] Her words are no understatement. Released in November 1960, *Hanyŏ* (*The Housemaid*) by Kim Ki-young (1919–98) encapsulated the mood of postwar South Korea, and its moment of profound social transformation. This impact, however, would not be felt until

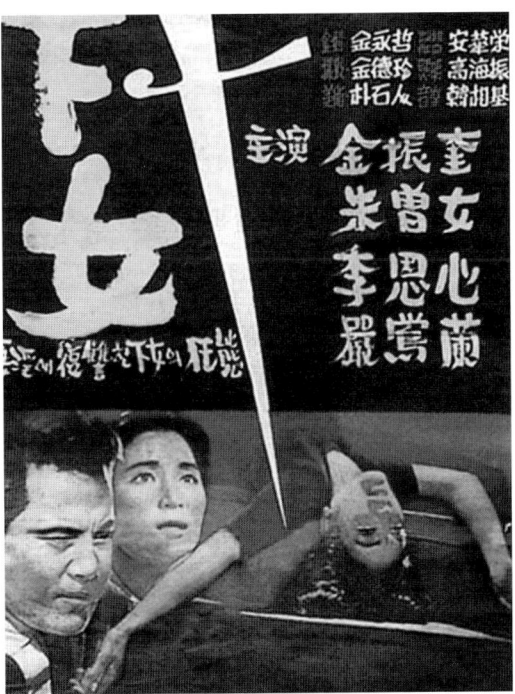

Hanyŏ poster, 1960 theatrical release

much later. Although a box-office hit when it premiered, *Hanyŏ* did not get the recognition it now enjoys – as one of the greatest Korean films ever – until Kim Ki-young's retrospective in 1997 at the Busan International Film Festival after decades of obscurity. From this later perspective, we can see how radically it broke from the nationalistic social realism that dominated contemporary Korean film-making at the time. While retaining a familiar melodramatic core, Kim turned a simple story – of a housemaid's affair with her employer – into an eye-opening tour de force of experimentation and vision. Kim culled from a wide array of influences: Surrealism, Dadaism, German Expressionism, Freudian psychoanalysis, Hollywood film noir, as well as Soviet avant-garde cinema and theatre. His varied cinematic aesthetic in turn reflected the highly vexed sensorium of a distressing historical period. These were times of tremendous upheaval and hasty transformation that followed on the heels of the devastating Korean War (1950–3), which literally divided families across a newly formed Cold War boundary. Korea had just recently emerged, still scarred, from three decades of Japanese colonialism (1910–45), only to find itself dependent on another global power. Under the wing of American authority, which viewed its prosperity as an important exemplar of western-style capitalism within a rapidly evolving global Cold War, South Korea emerged from postwar poverty with a mandate to industrialise and an imperative towards democracy.

In this dizzying context, a housemaid set loose on an upwardly mobile middle-class home became a monstrous embodiment of the destructive desires of capitalism, which recklessly undercut the foundations of tradition. An intrusive strider wishing for her own piece of an emergent prosperity, this femme fatale served as a cautionary tale amid the country's exuberant economic transformation, a transformation that would eventually earn South Korea praise as the 'miracle on the Han'. Against this triumphant discourse, the housemaid indexed a broad anxiety undergirding what might be otherwise regarded as a time of progress. *Hanyŏ* was released just a year before the inauguration of the authoritarian

The housemaid, monstrous embodiment of the destructive desires of modernity (courtesy Korean Film Archive)

government in 1961, which would shepherd two decades of state-led, export-driven industrialisation (1961–79). It registers more powerfully than any film of its period, in the figure of the female worker challenging Confucian gender norms, both the vigorous imperative towards radical transformation as well as its horrifying costs. It is significant that *Hanyŏ* arrived in theatres at the beginning of a period famously referred to as Korea's 'compressed modernity'[3]:

a civilizational condition in which economic, political, social, and/or cultural changes occur in an extremely condensed manner in respect to both time and space, and in which the dynamic coexistence of mutually disparate historical and social elements leads to the construction and reconstruction of a highly complex and fluid social system.[4]

The film reflects the deeply conflicted feelings of this historical moment.

While critics have frequently associated *Hanyŏ* generally with South Korea's rapid economic and social transition beginning in the

1960s, the film was a product of the very specific moment within Korean postwar history. *Hanyŏ* was released on 3 November 1960, just a few months after the 19 April Student Revolution toppled the regime of President Syngman Rhee, and a few months before Park Chung-hee's swift and bloodless military coup on 16 May 1961. This brief period is known as the Second Republic. It replaced the First Republic led by Rhee with the backing of the United States. Rhee had been instated in 1948 as president of the first indigenous government in Korea following the country's liberation from Japanese colonial rule in 1945. Despite US support, popular unrest surged as it became evident that Rhee's administration was not only ineffective in pushing through economic development, but also in democratising the political process and carrying out postwar reconstruction. Rhee's attempt to rig the electoral process to ensure his power incited nationwide protests, which fomented the revolution and hastened the end of the First Republic in April 1960.

The Second Republic was a time of both utopian thought and chaos. Rhee's government was followed by a three-month interim government, led by acting president Hŏ Chŏng. A democratic election was held in July 1960, leading to the formation of a parliamentary system, the nation's first and only experiment with such a system of government,[5] under President Yun Bo-sŏn and Prime Minister Chang Myŏn. This was a time when activists and politicians engaged in vigorous debate about the future of the country, a future that could now be determined by local actors rather than distant powers. Encouraged by a free press and a range of diverse views about planning and policy, the newly minted National Assembly was a space for creative thinking and possibility. This was also, however, a time of strenuous disagreement and ultimately discord, with debates becoming increasingly fractious rather than building towards consensus. As historian Bruce Cumings notes, 'few days passed without street demonstrations' during this tumultuous period.[6] Due to internecine feuding and indecisiveness, the new government ultimately failed to resolve problems left over by the

First Republic.[7] The Second Republic lasted only from April 1960 to May 1961. According to the historian Chun Soonok, the government was unsustainable because it 'contained an inherent ambivalence': it came to power via a popular revolution yet was fundamentally conservative, and thus incapable of addressing calls for radical change in domestic politics and international relations.[8]

However, the short-lived government did allow for a period of free expression in art and media, which made releasing a film as radical as *Hanyŏ* possible. Indeed, although it was written a few years earlier, *Hanyŏ* was produced during this period and released almost precisely at its mid-point, taking advantage of a June 1960 constitutional amendment, which included a provision for freedom of speech and assembly.[9] Both before and after this period, the government imposed official state censorship of popular media, including films. Within this milieu of utopian chaos, *Hanyŏ* boldly explored the social reorganisation that this as yet undetermined future might undertake, specifically in terms of class relations and how these emerging formations might be inflected in gender relations. And although the film begins in a factory employing an army of working women, its main preoccupation is with the scene of domesticity, the middle-class home.

It is crucial to understand that the middle class in South Korea in the world of *Hanyŏ* is still nascent, constituting less than 20 per cent of the population in 1960.[10] It grows rapidly from this point, rising to around 30 per cent by 1970 and over 50 per cent by 1995.[11] In this context, this book argues that *Hanyŏ* participated in imagining the formation of the middle class and its emerging subjectivities at the very beginning of compressed modernisation when the South Korean middle class was still a fledgling fantasy constructed by government-led campaigns. *Hanyŏ* is generally categorised with family melodramas in the so-called South Korean Golden Age of Melodramas of the 1960s, alongside films that were made after the end of the Second Republic, in a decade that indeed saw the rapid acceleration of many developments including the formation of the middle class. However, when *Hanyŏ* was released in November 1960, the concept of the middle class itself and its postwar formation was still in its early period of gestation. The film is thus not so much a dutiful reflection of existing class structures but more a fanciful projection of an emerging horizon, the nuclear family standing in as a 'symptomatic microcosm'[12] of the correlation between national community-building efforts and middle-class performativity. The outlook for South Korea looked very different from the perspective of the widespread economic poverty at the beginning of the decade than it did from the material wealth and prosperity at the end of that decade. *Hanyŏ* played a crucial role in the class imaginary leading up to the state-sponsored normative middle-class project and specific economic policy first articulated by the Park Chung-hee regime in 1961.[13]

Not grounded in an existing middle class as a dominant social formation, *Hanyŏ*'s narrative of middle-class anxieties and wealth takes great liberties. Kim Ki-young remade *Hanyŏ* several times between the 1960s and the 1980s, hoping to replicate its commercial success as well as advance his evolving aesthetic vision using new technologies such as colour. In an article published in the Korean film journal *CineForum* on the crucial historic moments of the middle class in South Korea as represented across Kim Ki-young's 'housemaid' series, Yi Dae-bŏm and Chŏng Su-wan argue that the housemaid films released in 1960, 1971 and 1982 are inflection points in compressed modernisation.[14] According to their periodisation of the formation of the middle class, the late 1950s to the mid-1960s was a preparational stage in which the economic foundations were laid to escape postwar poverty and hunger. The middle class was 'the goal of development, but the historical reality of the middle class was absent'.[15] This is a period when the 'romantic fantasy' of the middle class begins to stir under government-led slogans, and in which the material foundations of the postwar middle class begin to take shape. It is not until the late 1960s and early 1970s, as compressed modernisation gathers real momentum, that the 'realistic material foundation for the lifestyle of the middle class gets laid', coexisting alongside 'the ills of compressed modernity'.[16] Hagen Koo's periodisation of the formation of the middle class supports this timeline, arguing that the debate on 'the reality of the middle class' did not begin in earnest until 1966.[17] Yi and Chŏng's article focuses on the role of outsiders in the housemaid series, and in their analysis of Kim Ki-young's 1960 housemaid, they read *Hanyŏ* as both 'a symbol of utopia' and as a 'grid of collective delusion'.[18]

Focusing on the first and most famous of Kim's housemaid series, this book argues that *Hanyŏ*, more than simply depicting the middle class, participates in its imaginative *formation*, and accordingly in the formation of middle-class subjectivities in the public imagination. *Hanyŏ* expresses and then attempts to manage the tension that it derives from the sensorium of the Second Republic. Kim Ki-young would eventually go on to direct two explicit remakes of *Hanyŏ*, in *Hwanyŏ* (*Woman of Fire*, 1971) and *Hwanyŏ '82* (*Woman of Fire '82,* 1982), and commentators have argued that two of his other films – *Ch'ungnyŏ* (*The Insect Woman*, 1972) and *Yuksik tongmul* (*Carnivore*, 1984) – also qualify as remakes. In their study of *Hanyŏ* as part of a trilogy, Nikki Lee and Julian Stringer observe shifts in content and emphasis in the 1970s as Kim adapted to industry trends, most notably to a more 'melodramatic and emotional tone', settled notions of class and explanations for the housemaid's (referred to by her name Myŏng-ja in the remakes) psychological and social 'awakening to the power of sex' and morally deviant behaviour.[19] As the first of a series of films that explore similar stories involving housemaids, the original film served as a 'template' for these other versions.[20] Nevertheless, *Hanyŏ* of 1960 was the only film in Kim's career that gave him a sense of artistic ownership, referring to it as 'my film'.[21] The others, he felt, were compromised by a range of factors, including censorship and intrusive producers. It was also the first of his films to display the logo of his production company, the Korean Literature Film Company, a rising fist slowly opening to reveal the palm against a smoky background.

Kim Ki-young Productions logo

In its rediscovery and subsequent re-evaluation, *Hanyŏ* upset
the common perception that social realism was the sole aesthetic
that could fully manifest South Korean modernity. Here was a film,
released at the beginning of this modern moment, that unleashed a
far less restrained sensationalism, a sensorium of heightened affect.
Although it is true (as many commentators have pointed out) that
Hanyŏ was based on an actual murder case Kim had read about in
a newspaper, this basis in real events, along with the larger social
phenomenon of rural–urban migration and young women entering the
workforce, became an occasion for psychodrama rather than social
realism. Many have assumed that Kim used these actual events to lend

a realist basis to an otherwise erratic and fantastic tale, inferring the problems brought by rapid industrialisation and the entry of women's participation in the workforce. However, this realist framework is deceptive. In his groundbreaking work on Kim Ki-young's films, film scholar Chris Berry shows that the rediscovery of *Hanyŏ* radically overturned the largely unquestioned realist reputation of his pre-1980 films. In the 1980s, Kim churned out a string of largely unsuccessful 'over the top' flops, but because his older films were rarely shown on television (and his features made in the 1950s had not survived), he was still regarded among industry insiders, alongside Shin Sang-ok and Yu Hyun-mok, as one of the 'fathers of Korean realist cinema'.[22] Although cult film buffs had discovered some of Kim's older films on VHS, these were the later housemaid films and did not include *Hanyŏ*. When the films that had not been available on video were finally screened in the late 1990s, it became apparent that *Hanyŏ* marked a critical turning point away from realism.[23]

Berry argues against those critics that read the 'jealousy, adultery, ghosts, shamanism, rats, paranoia, sexual dysfunction, psychotic delusions, and gruesome murders' in Kim's films as critical or negative responses to modernisation, pointing instead to 'an ambivalent response to the Korean experience of modernization as at once forced and desired'. This 'paradoxical state', he argues, 'that defies either realist representation or critical distance prefers direct somatic response and full ambivalence'.[24] The erratic and incoherent quality of Kim's films, beginning with *Hanyŏ*, Berry claims, is symptomatic less of moral degeneration and more a shift towards the fantastic and horror. Such insight has led more recent critics to widely cite *Hanyŏ* as 'initiating the first cycle of modern Korean horror' and to refer to Kim Ki-young as 'Mr Monster' in recognition of his reputation 'as a master of horror'.[25] The 'direct somatic response' and preference for ambivalence suggests that a key aspect of *Hanyŏ*'s legacy is an acute awareness of film as a visceral and embodied medium, which helps remind us of what is lost in the disjunctive process of compressed modernisation.

The enduring value of *Hanyŏ*'s dark vision, however, is not just its uncanny aesthetics but also its politics. Although it was certainly not intended to be an explicitly feminist film, it would be remiss not to note the questions it raises about class mobility, gender oppression, power and women's labour. In this respect, it resonates strongly with contemporary feminist concerns regarding misogyny. Indeed, the power of the film – what Kim called its 'density' – is its deeply vexed treatment of social issues, seeming at once regressive in its demonisation of an unruly woman while at the same time valorising her sexualised exuberance. Even in this regard, the film was perhaps prescient, as the perpetuation of Confucian gender norms in the guise of capitalist growth is considered a key component in the success of South Korean industrialisation. Throughout the film, issues of class relations become complexly intertwined with other questions of inequality, which Korea's compressed modernisation only renders more pronounced, and which became even more pressing as, by the turn of the century, this period of high growth gave way to further difficult socio-economic circumstances in the twenty-first century.

Hanyŏ provides not only a text with which to examine the country's socio-political, cultural and gendered histories, and how these in turn cut across histories of representation, aesthetics and affect, but it also provides a lens for understanding the equally vexed condition of post-development Korea. The film postulates a material and corporeal basis as critical framework in its compressed, dense image, an inclination towards what Donna Haraway formulates as 'bodies as objects of knowledge' and 'material-semiotic generative nodes', whereby 'their boundaries materialize in social interaction'.[26] Materiality contributes to how discourses develop and transform.[27]

There is a curious regenerative capacity in *Hanyŏ* that has enabled its 'revival'[28] (via Kim Ki-young's own remakes), its revitalisation (via later iterations by other directors) and a sense of vitality (via the housemaid's 'resurrection' and extension into architectural embodiment). This regenerative capacity is also evident in its ability to accommodate a broad range of approaches, from class-based readings to new materialist interpretations. Film scholar Steve Choe sees a 'wild vitality' in Kim's animist aesthetics that accounts for a 'continuous production of difference' generated by the 'animative power of the moving image', which constantly imbues the original *Hanyŏ* with contemporary relevance.[29] Choe argues that the 'interpretative difficulties concerning the politics of representation' in the film seem to be insurmountable, especially when notions of sexual difference are associated with degrading non-human or animalistic traits (such as the housemaid with rats and the daughter with squirrels). To find a way out of this quandary, Choe turns to the 'vital life' Kim gives to non-human and inorganic life forms. Citing Kim Ki-young's own statements – that he sought to reveal 'everything that lay hidden' and 'tried to show the facts and the truth anatomically'[30] – Choe wonders if perhaps this includes the life of inanimate objects in the film and 'the material and affective relations between bodies in the world'. Ultimately, it seems, the distinctions between human and non-human beings (such as animals) 'aim toward dissolution'.[31]

After having been nearly lost, *Hanyŏ* has become the object of reverence as an important artistic rendering of the transition that led to Korean modernity by a new generation of Korean directors such as Park Chan-wook, Im Sang-soo, Kim Ki-duk, Ryu Seung-wan, Kim Jee-woon and Bong Joon Ho, who has referred to *Hanyŏ* as 'the *Citizen Kane* of Korean cinema'. Kim Ki-young played a formative part in what is known as South Korean cinema's 'Golden Age' of the 1960s and 1970s, alongside directors Sin Sang-ok, Yi Man-hee and Han Hyŏng-mo, all of whom defined Korean postwar realism. After breaking into film-making while working for the United States Information Service (USIS) following the Korean War with the film short *Nanŭn t'ŭrŏgida* (*I Am a Truck*, 1952), Kim debuted with the anti-communist *Chugŏmŭi sangja* (*Box of Death*, 1955), the first Korean film to use synchronous sound, and the feature *Yangsando* (*Yangsan Province*, 1955). *Hanyŏ* marked a new phase in his career characterised by a turn towards the psychological and expressionistic. Although Kim eschewed any kind of '-isms' or

Kim Ki-young (courtesy Kim Dong-yang, Kim Ki-young's family)

the desire to 'affix anything like that to my stuff', he brought to *Hanyŏ* various styles of film-making and influences, including Freudian psychoanalysis, German Expressionism and Surrealism, attesting to an experimental engagement with cinemas beyond those of Korea and Hollywood that was ahead of his time.

Hanyŏ is now widely acknowledged as one of the most important films in Korean cinema and a pinnacle of Korean Golden Age cinema. However, while it is most familiar, it has also accomplished this familiarity in relative obscurity. After its initial run, *Hanyŏ* remained unreleased on VHS and unseen for decades because it was missing two of its ten reels. It was only recovered when an original negative owned by Kim Ki-young's family was brought to the attention of the Korean Film Archive (KOFA) in 1982. In the 1960s, negatives were commonly discarded by production companies when films left theatres, and celluloid film was often used as a popular material to stiffen men's hats. Had the film not been produced with the director's private funds, it is likely that a copy would not have survived. A subtitled print made in 1960 for international film festival release was discovered in the 1990s and used to replace the missing reels, and in 1997, the Busan International Film Festival held a highly anticipated Kim Ki-young retrospective, showcasing a restored version of *Hanyŏ*. It then underwent a high-profile restoration process to remove the burned-in subtitles in collaboration with archivists, computer scientists, digital film laboratories and with funding from the World Cinema Foundation, just in time for its premiere at the Cannes Film Festival in 2008.[32] Subsequently, it was added to the Criterion Collection in 2013 and is now widely accessible to global audiences.

Before it was rediscovered, however, the film existed only in memories and written accounts. Film-makers and cinephiles could only view various remakes on extant VHS copies. Thus, although his overall popularity faded amid the challenges posed to Korean film-making by the military dictatorship, competition with Hollywood films and the growing popularity of television, the director re-emerged to become a cult hero during the 1980s and 1990s on the strength of the limited material that remained in circulation. As a result, Kim Ki-young has remained an important and appreciated Korean director. He has been compared to Luis Buñuel for his incisive treatment of desire; to Alfred Hitchcock for his continuous recycling of tropes that gave his oeuvre more cohesion; and to Ingmar Bergman for his background in theatre directing. Due in part to this cult following, the rediscovery of *Hanyŏ* created a sensation. Following on the heels of the restoration in 2010, director Im Sang-soo remade *Hanyŏ*, and followed it with a sequel of sorts, *Ton ŭi mat* (*The Taste of Money*, 2012), which reimagined the role of the housemaid as a male corporate employee working in the home of an entirely different wealthy family. Most recently, director Bong Joon Ho repeatedly credited *Hanyŏ* as a source of inspiration for his film *Kisaengch'ung* (*Parasite*, 2019) during its successful run through the Cannes Film Festival and the Academy Awards.

1 Tension and Censorship

Hanyŏ centres on a young woman who leaves her job in a textile
factory to become a housemaid (played by Yi Ŭn-sim). Even among
the female factory workers, she is marginalised: whereas the other
women make textiles, her job is to clean. Because of her role in the
factory, she is recommended for the position of housemaid in a
middle-class home to assist the music teacher's wife, Jŏng-sim (played
by Chu Jŭng-nyŏ), a seamstress who is pregnant. Importantly, the
home is a new, modern two-storey house, with the family living on
the ground floor and the housemaid occupying a room upstairs,
across the landing from the room where the music teacher, Dong-sik
(played by veteran actor Kim Jin-kyu), works as a composer and gives
piano lessons. Dong-sik teaches both at the factory and in his home,
and his students include the women factory workers themselves. We
should note from the outset the off-kilter nature of these depictions: a
piano teacher as an emblem of middle-class affluence (possibly from
the upper class, given Dong-sik's ownership of a piano) and well-
dressed factory girls who are unusually polished and engage in leisure
pursuits like music lessons as an extension of their factory work.
Differentiated from this class of young women who seem destined
for the middle class despite their current occupations, the housemaid,
naive and uneducated, is a representative figure of the wave of young
women who migrated from rural villages to the city in the period to
find employment in factories but were often forced to work instead as
bus conductresses, barmaids or prostitutes. These types of jobs were
often associated with a dangerous sexuality, which posed a threat to
Korea's sense of propriety.

    Hanyŏ's two female leads came from very different acting
backgrounds, a difference that Kim emphasised by establishing stark
contrasts in his shot compositions and sequences. In an essay he

published in the film journal *Kukje Yŏnghwa* (International Film) in August 1960 shortly before the release of *Hanyŏ*, entitled 'Chu Jŭng-nyŏ's Performance and Life', Kim Ki-young writes in detail about his reasons for casting Chu, who was already a veteran actress, in the role of Jŏng-sim. Jŏng-sim works diligently at a sewing machine in the workroom on the ground floor next to their bedroom, to help pay for the family's purchase of their new house. Driven by the pursuit of middle-class luxuries, she works to the point of neglecting her family and sacrificing her health. A single-minded, determined character, the role of Jŏng-sim required a steadfast performance.

Chu came from a theatre background, and Kim Ki-young had wanted to cast her in a film ever since he first directed her in a stage production of Ibsen's *Ghosts*. He wrote, 'From the start, when I was writing the screenplay for *Hanyŏ*, the female lead character, Yi Jŏng-sim, was written to set up Chu Jŭng-nyŏ as the "heroine".'[33] The 'quiet yet elegant aura of [Chu's] performance' strongly appealed to Kim and reminded him of the Hollywood actress Deborah Kerr, who at the peak of her stardom in the 1950s had been featured on the cover of several Korean film magazines. In *Hanyŏ*, Kim hoped that Chu would emulate Ingrid Bergman's Oscar-winning performance in the paranoia-filled film noir *Gaslight* (dir. George Cukor, 1944), in which she plays a rich and sheltered woman trapped in her house by her husband, who terrorises her and has an affair with the young maid. Of Chu, Kim wrote,

In whatever role she is given, the scene's atmosphere created by Chu is emotional. Even when given a lustful role or a shameful role, she has a way in which she does not lose her unique charm of having the atmosphere physically somehow [embrace] her emotionally and elegantly.[34]

Her 'screen face' harmonised stage and film acting in a way that he found perfectly suited the role of Jŏng-sim, a role that required emotional restraint, particularly in 'situations in which [Jŏng-sim] intermittently works through these surging feelings and indignation'.[35] Kim would rely on Chu to produce a realistic performance of the character's increasing anxieties.

In contrast, Kim did not have a specific actress in mind for the role of the housemaid, and wanted someone unknown who would complement Chu's wealth of experience. Kim published an account of casting new actresses – his 'Star Theory' – in a special issue of *Wolgan Yŏnghwa* (*The Monthly Cinema*) in December 1984, titled 'Adventures Regarding New Actresses'.[36] He was very conscious that inexperienced actresses often found it difficult to relax in front of the camera, which could make it tricky for audiences to empathise; but he also ruminated considerably on how best to foster skilled acting from them.[37] Kim eventually cast Yi Ŭn-sim, who had appeared in a minor role in his *Sŭlp'ŭn mokka* (*A Sad Pastorale*, 1960), but was relatively unknown. The contrast in actor experience ultimately proved useful to the dynamic between the two women. The housemaid's unstable, disruptive presence serves as a foil to Jŏng-sim's consistent resolve, particularly as the tension builds between them. Although an exception to Kim's preference for actors who worked in the Stanislavski method, Yi, in her inexperience, embodied the role of the ingenuous and ambitious maid who adapts and transforms by mimicking those around her.

In *Hanyŏ*, the housemaid's sexuality threatens the sanctity of the middle-class home, but this is learned behaviour that she acquires by witnessing another factory girl (Kyŏng-hŭi, played by Ŏm Aeng-ran) attempt to seduce Dong-sik, a married father of two children, during a piano lesson. This is an important element of the plot because it suggests that the housemaid's sexuality is comparative by nature and not intrinsic; it is desire modelled on someone else's desire, a form of imitation. That the housemaid's desire requires a model indexes a historical moment in which class formations are still nascent. It is not simply that she desires entry into the middle class; rather, it is as if she needs to discover what to desire in the first place. The factory girl's failed seduction not only suggests a method of access to the class occupied by the piano teacher's family, but it is also an articulation of

'Feather your nest'

what the appropriate objects of desire might be. Soon after witnessing the failed seduction, the housemaid successfully forces Dong-sik into a quick and tumultuous affair that takes place within the confines of the once idyllic middle-class home and soon results in her pregnancy. Furthermore, the housemaid's imitation of a previously expressed desire reflects a core characteristic of middle-class expansion – with aspirants wanting the same kind of mass-produced home, vehicle and products enjoyed by their neighbours. Indeed, this sort of imitative consumerism has served as a core tenet of capitalist middle-class ideology. The housemaid's imitative desire, however, operates in an economy of scarcity in which one cannot find one's own husband and a house next door but rather must poach from a limited inventory, making her all the more threatening.

The home, in turn, becomes a site of conflict and competition. Jŏng-sim, seeing her own standing in the family threatened by the housemaid's grip on her husband, forces her to abort the child. Jŏng-sim is also pregnant, a fact that makes clear the housemaid's actions cannot be thought of as anything other than usurpation. Chaos ensues. Angered by the family's abuse, the vengeful housemaid kills their young son and, in the dramatic climax of the film, forces Dong-sik to kill himself by taking rat poison with her. This is a cautionary tale that ultimately valorises the normative, upwardly mobile middle-class family, but one that does so by dwelling in the threatening disorder that the housemaid creates.

Responding perhaps to these paradoxical imperatives, the newspaper *Tonga Ilbo*'s review of *Hanyŏ*, published on 9 November 1960, a week after its release, was ambivalent, describing the film as 'a failed attempt but noteworthy experiment'.[38] Even though the review complimented the film for not abandoning 'the experimental spirit of putting the camera on human psychology',[39] it was ultimately critical of its unsatisfying vision of reality, criticising the film for its over-the-top sensibility, rough portrayals of character motivation and uneven plot. But if the film was overblown by realist criteria, Kim Ki-young aimed for a different standard of verisimilitude targeted instead at the inchoate sensorium of the tumultuous period of the Second Republic. Of the view that 'in large part, the background and mood of the period are what determine a film',[40] Kim likened his own approach to film-making to François Truffaut's *Les Quatre Cents Coups* (*The 400 Blows*, 1959). Kim was drawn to the film's expression of the period's nuclear anxiety in France through the lens of an adolescent's experience, which he saw as palpably rendering the psychological state of distress to audiences and eliciting their empathy.

Using *Les Quatre Cents Coups* as an example, Kim stated that a great film 'must always contain the circumstances of the time as a "*plus alpha*" ... When you know the reality, you know where the film is headed.'[41] The expression 'plus alpha' is borrowed here possibly from Japanese English, and refers to an added bonus, profit or effect. It also suggests a willingness to risk a certain excessiveness to express more forcefully the urgencies of a particular historical moment. A discourse of happiness and technologies of self-care had emerged in the late 1950s, partly in response to postwar poverty, crime, high rates of suicide, and widespread anxiety related to material dissatisfaction and fear of mental illness.[42] *Hanyŏ*'s 'plus alpha' is achieved through a taut internal structure that represents the political tension of this interstitial period and the sensorium of the Second Republic via psychological horror and suspense. In so doing, the film produces a pronounced – and sustained – tension between reality and fantasy, between anxiety and happiness, an appropriate cocktail for a period that had to balance the need for practical policy-making against the promise of utopian futures. *Hanyŏ* maintains this tenuous balance by grounding its fantastical elements in the realities of the moments from which they emerge, with the film's pulsing undercurrent emerging from the psychological impacts of modernisation, urbanisation and industrialisation, all of which were felt during the Second Republic but perhaps not yet clearly articulated. At the same time, this sensorium of the Second Republic is one of surprise, embodied by the housemaid. She comes from nowhere, with no backstory, and emerges out of a closet. The housemaids of Kim's later remakes of *Hanyŏ* are socially situated, but here, her sudden emergence, full of possibility but also danger, *is* the essence of modernity in 1960.

Hanyŏ's narrative tension holds 'fantasy' in abeyance, lodged in the film's overall structure as a liminal state between a beginning and end posited as 'reality' that exerts relentless pressure on the unfolding events. Working with the film composer Han Sang-ki (1917–2004), who collaborated with Kim throughout his career, Kim injected a mood of fear and tension into the taut narrative structure of the film by playing with the movement of the camera and sound. Discordant piano sounds and atonal music characteristic of horror films are used to heightened effect in pivotal scenes, image and sound working in tandem to generate a strained atmosphere. Although Kim continued to experiment with creating an atmosphere of horror and a sense of depth in his later remakes of *Hanyŏ*, he relied more on the colour technology that was becoming available instead of sound, marking what he saw as a notable change in his style.[43] The inextricable relationship established between sound and image to create tension is most pronounced in the original *Hanyŏ*, the sounds of modernisation such as the machinery at the factory, the piano, the sewing machine, the rain and thunder variously attuned to the ongoing spatial

conflicts in the house. At the start of the film, the discordant music of
the scene in the family room contrasts with the sound of inclement
weather outside, initiating the film's tension. As the narrative
progresses, music is increasingly connected to the objects of fear (rats
and the housemaid), until it recedes in the final stage, giving way to
only the sound of rain to 'create melancholy and despair rather than
tension'.[44] In a way, Kim's approach to encapsulating the tension
of the times as 'plus alpha' resonates with what Michel Chion calls
'added value', defined as 'the expressive and informative value with
which a sound enriches a given image',[45] in a mutually formative
relationship between visual and auditory perception.

As alluded to in the opening of the film, *Hanyŏ* was based on
an actual murder case. Sitting in their living room, Dong-sik and
Jŏng-sim read aloud a newspaper article about a housemaid who
killed her employers that was based on real-life events. In the town
of Gimchŏn, a housemaid had drowned her employer's five-year-old
son in a pond after their affair. There was also the case in Changwŏn
where a housemaid had killed the couple that employed her.[46]
Such news stories incited fear (as in the film) about the intrusion of
threatening women into people's homes at a time when the middle-
class household was becoming fetishised as an emergent object

Dong-sik and Jŏng-sim read a newspaper article about a
murderous housemaid

of desire. *Hanyŏ* intensifies and clearly expresses such anxieties. A particular locus for these anxieties was the rural–urban migration of young girls who came to Seoul 'without any definite plans in mind' – a phenomenon that Kim suggested was central to the 'reality of this film'.[47]

String of tension

If, as I have suggested, the Second Republic was ultimately an interstitial moment in Korean history – a time of utopian possibility and radical uncertainty – Kim Ki-young carefully developed for *Hanyŏ* an enigmatic principle that he called the 'string of tension' [*kinjangŭi kkŭn*] to express the period's paradoxical investments in reality and fantasy. He believed that, as the director, he was responsible for holding taut a metaphorical string that stood for all the contradictory elements that composed its world.[48] In its opening moments, in fact, *Hanyŏ* offers a literal version of this principle. As the opening credits roll, we see the brother and sister playing cat's cradle, looping and re-looping in increasingly complicated ways the string intertwined between their fingers. The string's tension is in turn doubled in the taut relation Kim creates between darkness and light in the title shot's composition. The large bold white lettering of *Hanyŏ* in Chinese script that appears on the screen as the children

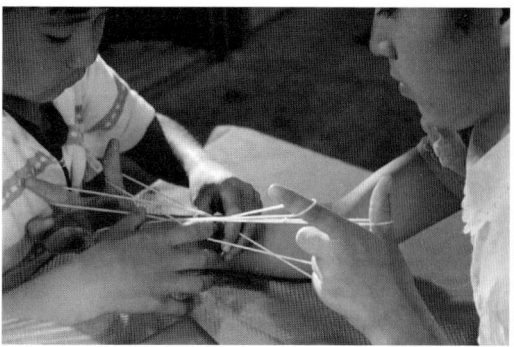

Playing cat's cradle

Hanyŏ title with bloody lettering in Chinese script

continue their game drips creepily at the bottom of each letter 'like blood', a touch that Kim Ki-young drew by hand himself. The stark white lettering in turn contrasts sharply with the darkness that otherwise pervades the scene. From the outset, the scene establishes the motif of contrast between light and shadow that remains consistently throughout the film – a motif that implies a sense of anxiety heightened by the discordant piano music.[49]

Literalised in the opening scene, Kim's string of tension also emerges in the psychological entanglements of characters and is amplified by the film's generic commitment to melodrama, a genre designed precisely to dramatise and indeed exaggerate social tensions.[50] In an interview, Kim offered the example of the factory girl Kyŏng-hŭi, and her calculated manipulation of both another worker, Kwak Sŏn-yŏng (Ko Sŏn-ae), and the housemaid, each of whom she tries to use as pawns in her failed plan to seduce Dong-sik.[51] Although she quickly disappears from the narrative frame, the plot's central story of Dong-sik's downfall is in fact set in motion by Kyŏng-hŭi's machinations. She has a crush on Dong-sik and so uses her friend and co-worker Sŏn-yŏng to assess the impact of the potential repercussions of a love confession. Kyŏng-hŭi convinces Sŏn-yŏng to leave a love note for Dong-sik on the piano during a music lesson at the factory. Unmoved, he reports the incident, resulting in Sŏn-yŏng's suspension. Forced to return home, she gets sick and dies. It is also Kyŏng-hŭi who recommends the housemaid for employment in the Kims' home, going so far as to offer an additional one-fifth of the wages out of her own pocket to convince the hesitant housemaid to take the position.

These narrative threads about manipulated women are held together formally by repeated medium shots of Kyŏng-hŭi, with a sombre but determined expression on her face, crossing the street towards the Kims' house as a train (that classic figure of modernity) passes behind her. The first shot occurs after she sees Sŏn-yŏng off at the train station following her suspension, and the second when Kyŏng-hŭi comes to the Kims' house for piano lessons. Ultimately, her own seduction of Dong-sik fails when he rejects her violently, but her attempts at seduction serve as models for the observant housemaid. We see here the tension in Kim's string at work, with the force increasingly intensified. The threat to the household is established through the initial forays of these minor characters, only to be followed through in greater force by the housemaid. After Sŏn-yŏng and Kyŏng-hŭi's failures, the housemaid proves to be a more formidable seductress, and thus amplifies in a crescendo-like structure the original more modest tensions with which the film begins.

Repeated shot of the train, a symbol of modernity, behind Kyŏng-hŭi as she goes to the Kims' house

Kyŏng-hŭi seduces Dong-sik

The film thus builds mounting pressure in the recursive series of seduction attempts, each temptation harder for Dong-sik to resist than the one before, not least because the stain of the past seductions accrues. The housemaid in fact blackmails Dong-sik with knowledge of the false rape accusation and suicide that Kyŏng-hŭi had threatened (but did not carry out). She demands that Dong-sik stay with her in her room, in retribution for Jŏng-sim forcing her to abort her pregnancy. Belying Kyŏng-hŭi's initial description of her as 'a bit of an idiot', the housemaid proves instinctive in adapting to her environment in opportunistic ways. Her actions are frightening precisely because they emerge from the upwardly mobile ethos that the film otherwise seems to valorise. She is both a threat to the emergent middle-class sensibility expressed in the film and, as an ambitious social climber, its ideal subject.

Perhaps the most dramatic example of Kim Ki-young's attempt to sustain tension in *Hanyŏ* is its famous framing device. Although the majority of the film was originally shot in chronological sequence, Kim Ki-young later added the opening and closing scenes that remain untouched by the housemaid's violent disturbance of domestic bliss. A symmetrical bracket around the tragic central story, these scenes reframe the film's primary diegesis in proto-postmodern fashion as a cautionary tale that perhaps never actually happened. Established in

Opening scene: entering the house through the window

the opening scene, the camera enters from the outside of the house through a window into the room where the Kim family is spending the evening. Dong-sik points out a newspaper story to Jŏng-sim about a man who had an affair with the family's housemaid. Jŏng-sim is disturbed by the idea. In turn, the closing sequence of the film picks up where the opening scene left off: the wife puts down the newspaper and expresses her disapproval. Although we have just seen her die, the housemaid is alive now and once again subservient, coming into the living room to serve the family refreshments. To assuage our confusion, Dong-sik turns to the audience, breaking the fourth wall to let us know that the story we have just witnessed was an imagined cautionary tale against the kind of moral depravity suggested in such newspaper articles. Then, the film suddenly ends, and we are left to wonder whether all this actually happened, or was just a dream, or something else.

There will be more to say about the precipitous ending of the film and the strange visual elements buried therein in Chapter 2, but for now I want to emphasise the ambivalence in the framing device between the way it functions to disrupt narrative continuity and the way Kim Ki-young uses formal continuities to counterbalance the frame's disjunctive effect. At the beginning of the film, following the previously discussed opening credits over the children's cat's cradle

Cut to textile factory; framed by spools: Kyŏng-hŭi and
Sŏn-yŏng keep thread taut at the weaving machine

game, the scene cuts to the textile factory floor, where rows of large
loud machines weave thread into fabric. Kim Ki-young employs here
a *narratage* technique (in which a character in the role of storyteller
supplements the actual story) to transition from Dong-sik discussing
the newspaper article in the opening sequence to the subsequent
depiction of the housemaid's story. This cut to the factory seems to
be just a straightforward shift in space, from the house to the factory
floor, but we learn that the cut is also a shift in time, to a past before
their move to the new house. Although we eventually appreciate
this temporal shift, it does not register as a shift into an alternative
counterfactual narrative realm; this feels like simply an earlier

View of the housemaid's dead body from outside the window; cut to the moving train

moment in the world depicted in the film's opening, not an alternative hypothetical trajectory.

Similarly, just before the closing frame, the camera pulls seamlessly back from a view of the housemaid's dead body on the staircase to a view of the body from outside the window, before cutting to a shot of a passing train. The noise of the train continues – doubling the sound of the mechanical loom that ends the opening sequence – as the camera moves from the outside back into the Kims' house and to Jŏng-sim reading the newspaper. This movement of the camera indoors through the balcony window reverses the direction of the camera moving outdoors in the prior shot of the

Jŏng-sim reading the newspaper inside the piano room

housemaid's corpse, and parallels its movement through the window
to the interior of the home at the beginning of the film. Although
the sequence is not continuous, as it is interrupted by the shot of the
train, the symmetry of the camera movement from inside to outside
and back inside belies the narrative disjuncture that is confirmed by
the sight of the housemaid in the room alive again. Thus, although
the film's framing device sits in disjunctive narrative relationship
to the rest of the plot, the film is careful to connect these disparate
diegeses through formal means, ultimately signalling a strange
ambivalence between a story of what had actually happened and

The housemaid is still alive

a story about what could have happened but, much to our relief, did not. We may think of this odd combination – formal continuity and ontological uncertainty – in relation to the very strange year in Korean history that was the Second Republic. As with the ambivalent framing device, modernity in 1960 seems at once disjunctive and disruptive, caught in a moment of track switching that unsettles our certainties and renders the way forward opaque, but also rife with possibility, offering the promise of progress and prosperity long denied a nation mired in colonial brutality, war and poverty.

Some critics have speculated about whether Kim Ki-young's decision to add the framing device was a consequence of concern over censorship, while others have suggested that it was primarily a stylistic choice, possibly influenced by the dream sequence in Robert Wiene's film *Das Cabinet des Dr. Caligari* (*The Cabinet of Dr. Caligari*, 1920). For his own part, Kim Ki-young would later insist that adding the opening and closing scenes was a decision he made because he simply didn't like the original version. In Yu Ji-hyŏng's famous interviews with Kim, *24 Years of Conversation* (published in 2006), the director and screenwriter asks Kim to clarify. Kim replies that the film's material was indeed shocking and potentially impactful, but that, as he saw it, 'at the time, it was also a hopeful message for the audience. The audience's disappointment would have been enormous if this model family, and the success it created through sewing and piano tutoring, were destroyed'.[52] To have the Kims' efforts undermined by the housekeeper, he felt, would have given audiences a 'futile conclusion'. For Kim Ki-young, the new structure communicated instead the message that 'a person who seeks happiness is filled with hope again from a brief nightmare. Such a form fit the current trend of the time, and it can be said that the form was successful.'[53] Thus, the film contains a built-in ambivalence, even as the framing device attempts to resolve that ambivalence by restoring order under the guise of 'reality'.

Modernity ultimately fails the housemaid, but at least as represented in the start of the film, it appears salutary. Hard work is

Jŏng-sim regrets material desires

rewarded by a big house, a large television and indeed, a housemaid. As the narrative progresses, however, Kim Ki-young's vision of modernity incorporates the ills of the feudal past into a debased capitalist form, full of horrific entrapments. Korean modernity becomes a warped version of western modernity, perpetuating existing discriminatory and gendered oppressions while also generating new ones.[54] If the rearrangement of the film's overall structure through the addition of the framing device turns everything that happened in the Kim household – from the circumstances necessitating the housemaid's employment to her eventual death by double suicide – into a fantasy, the reality that we are left with nevertheless portends the fate explored in the fantasy. In this way, the film exemplifies Kim Ki-young's way of seeing a world in tension between reality and fantasy, within which there were unpredictable transgressions between the dictates of society and the instincts of nature, and between ethics and primal desire.

Censorship window

The tension that the film thematises in various ways also reflects its pre-release history. *Hanyŏ* was considered shocking for its time, due to its depictions of infanticide, double suicide and adultery. Until recently, there has been a great deal of speculation regarding the extent to which the film was censored, and why so much was not censored given the conditions at the time. In June 2022, the Korean Film Archive released censorship data ranging from the mid-1950s to the mid-1990s pertaining to Kim Ki-young, including permits and handwritten memos, as part of their digitally accessible 'Censored Data Collection'.[55] The materials provide information for twenty-four of the thirty-two films Kim Ki-young completed before his tragic death in 1998. Due to the grotesque, sexually explicit and generally controversial subject matter of his films, Kim's works were heavily impacted by government censorship, especially from the mid-1970s to the early 1980s, under the stringent policies of South Korea's successive military dictatorships. During this period, Kim was forced to re-edit his films heavily. *Pan Kŭmnyŏn* (*The Story of Pan Kŭmnyŏn*, 1981), for example, a historical drama set in ancient China based on the novel of manners *Jin Ping Mei* (translated into English as *The Plum in the Golden Vase*), was rejected four times, across five years of edits, for its explicit depictions of sexuality. Although *Pan Kŭmnyŏn* was written in 1974, it was not released until 1981 after Kim Ki-young had cut forty minutes from his original version. Aside from sexual content, other films – such as *Nŭmi* (*The Deaf Worker*, 1980) and *Minyŏ Hong Nang-ja* (*Lady Hong, the Beauty*, 1969) – were censored due to concerns about the promotion of superstition and depiction of revenge scenes that were deemed excessive.

The censorship documentation on *Hanyŏ* consists of thirty-nine pages and includes 'Domestic Film Screening Reports' for the period from 1 November 1960 (just before its release) to 31 October 1963. Here, there is no mention of infanticide, sexual assault, suicide by poisoning or adultery. The 1 November report suggests that the film's perceived impact lay less with its excessive and violent content and more with its message of repentance. The series of stamps and signatures show that the application for a screening permit submitted by Kim Ki-young's Korean Literature Film Company moved through the official channels via the Korean Film Producers Association

[*Hanguk Yŏnghwa Chejakka Hyŏbhwe*] to the Ministry of Education
(MoE) [*Munkyobu*], which was in charge of administering motion
picture censorship from 1955 to 1961.[56] In the document, certain
words have been crossed out in red, indicating that forms from
before the April Revolution were being reused under the new
administration. Because official state censorship had been abolished
under the Second Republic and replaced with a gentler review
process, the phrase 'screening permission' has been crossed out and
replaced with 'screening report'. The 'restrictions' column, which
would under the old regime contain a list of censored elements, has
also been deleted in red pen.[57] This document shows that *Hanyŏ* was
not flagged for censorship issues, and that it was rated, as expected,
for mature audiences but was otherwise deemed 'unharmful'. The
report summarises *Hanyŏ*'s plot as follows: 'The content is about
a man with a happy family who has an extra-marital affair with a
housemaid and then repents for his crime by committing double-
suicide by poison with the housemaid.'

Screening permits after the April Revolution were governed by
the newly formed civilian National Motion Picture Ethics Committee
(NMPEC) [*Yŏnghwayunri chŏngukwiwŏnhoe*], South Korea's 'first
autonomous regulation agency free from state intervention'.[58] The
NMPEC is often cited by Korean film scholars such as Hye Seung
Chung as 'the primary reason why several of the most socially
conscious masterpieces of South Korean cinema, such as *The
Housemaid* [Hanyŏ] (1960), *The Coachman*, and *The Stray Bullet*
[*Aimless Bullet*], all arrived between August 1960 and May 1961, a
short period when the committee was existent'.[59] A departure from
a far more repressive state apparatus, while the civilian NMPEC was
nominally 'responsible for film censorship', it was guided by more
open-minded principles, basing

its regulations on the premise of 'freedom of speech and art creation.'
It emphasized the observance of a democratic constitution and the
deference of humanism. Although the Committee lasted little more than

a year and was disbanded soon after the military coup, it has been regarded as the only civilian organization overseeing content moderation in the history of Korean film.[60]

Their exact process is unknown, but we do know that this committee of experts reviewed every film that applied for a screening permit, and that those films that were deemed 'problematic' – again, for reasons that aren't entirely clear – were then studied further by one of several subcommittees.[61]

Despite the new emphasis on free speech, the NMPEC had to consider moral standards and public perception, so it did not simply rubber-stamp the films it reviewed. The tricky nature of the NMPEC's responsibilities in fact became evident about a month before *Hanyŏ* was released, when critics and public opinion began to oppose the screening of Louis Malle's *Les Amants* (*The Lovers*, 1958), due to its perceived immorality and obscenity. By film historian Cho Junhyoung's account, the MoE announced on 4 October that it would suspend the screening of the film in Korea, testing the authority of the NMPEC, and on 18 October that a decision about the film would be determined not through the NMPEC but through customs laws governing imports.[62] Similar problems arose with films such as Marc Allégret's *L'Amant de Lady Chatterley* (*Lady Chatterley's Lover*, 1955), which had been banned in New York because it was thought to promote adultery, and was released only in 1959 after the US Supreme Court overturned a lower court's decision; and the Italian films *Rosso e nero* (dir. Domenico Paolella, 1954) and *La tempesta* (*Tempest*, dir. Alberto Lattuada, 1958).[63] Considering that *Hanyŏ* shared some of the same features with these other films, the MoE's decision did not bode well for its release. And although the emergence of the NMPEC during the Second Republic signalled a departure from the previous government's censorship efforts, its ongoing clash with the MoE effectively kept at least some prospect of censorship on the table.[64]

Fortunately for *Hanyŏ*, the MoE's stance was fiercely challenged by the film industry, the media and the NMPEC, which saw the crackdown as a 'revival of the film censorship system'.[65] The MoE denied these charges, asserting that 'due diligence' was necessary to assess the content of a film being considered for import. The film industry argued that because the MoE required a recommendation letter for a film to be imported, importers voluntarily deleted parts of films they thought the MoE would disapprove of. These pre-emptive edits, it argued, were no different from government inspection and censorship.[66] Even in the immediate weeks before *Hanyŏ*'s release, it was not yet clear if the film would be censored. On 26 October 1960, the newspaper *Kyunghyang Sinmun* reported that the MoE's preventative measures to block the import of 'adultery currency' [*bullyunŭi waehwa*] were necessary to stem 'the tide of adultery films following the April Revolution' and 'in light of the reality that morality [*doŭi*] had fallen to the ground, causing mounting social chaos'.[67] Certainly, although it was obviously not an import, *Hanyŏ* contained elements that were cause for concern for the MoE. The 27 July 1960 report, however, ultimately verifies that *Hanyŏ* did not officially run afoul of any censorship measures and was deemed 'unharmful'.

Along with *Hanyŏ*, the other film most associated with this post-April Revolution period and the NMPEC's impact is Yu Hyŏn-mok's *Obalt'an* (*Aimless Bullet*, 1961). A comparison of this film, which was heavily impacted by censorship and a two-year ban from 1961 to 1963, with the treatment *Hanyŏ* received suggests that a fundamental distinction between the state's approach to the two films lay in the perceived degree of difference in their 'tonal incompatibility with the new government's cultural policy of cheerful national uplift' and their capacity to 'foster a particular mode of affirmative emotions while discouraging negative feelings through the affective monitoring of national cinema'.[68] As mentioned earlier, Kim Ki-young's decisions regarding the structural changes to *Hanyŏ* and the narrative turn took into consideration whether the film would ultimately be uplifting to viewers. As such, his changes were already consistent with the pervading sense cemented later by the Park Chung-hee administration's film policy enforcing a cinema of cheerful 'national uplift' and in line with the state's goals of modernisation and nation-building.[69]

Like *Hanyŏ*, *Obalt'an* has a large collection of recently released censorship documents, some of which indirectly reveal the close calls *Hanyŏ* had with censorship. The 'Domestic Film Screening Report' for *Obalt'an* – filed on 14 February 1961, a few months before the coup – shows it went through the same NMPEC regulatory review as *Hanyŏ*, but in contrast to *Hanyŏ*, it contains an 'examination commentary' written by the NMPEC, with instructions that a 'shot in which a woman hanging with a child on her back in the sewer passage of Gaech'ŏn' be cut.[70] More generally, *Obalt'an* had also encountered problems due to its perceived gloomy depiction of the depressing conditions of postwar Korea, and the film struggled to find financial backing. After the revolution, Yu was finally able to raise the production costs and complete *Obalt'an* by February 1961; and following the NMPEC's review process, it was released in April 1961. But this, too, was to be a brief victory.

On 16 May 1961, martial law was declared after a *coup d'état* led by Park Chung-hee. Censorship was revived almost immediately, including an order to re-censor works that had already been cleared for screening by the NMPEC. On 23 May 1961, the Ministry of Interior (MoI) [*Naemubu*] sent the MoE a list of thirty-five Korean films and twenty-two foreign films released after 1958 that the new Park government had classified as 'impure'. The results were filed in a separate document prepared by the film department of the Ministry of Public Information (MPI) [*Kongbobu*], which now handled film censorship instead of the MoE as a consolidation of all film regulatory activities under a single administrative and state-controlled unit. The document shows that the fifty-seven 'impurity films' were narrowed down to a total of three domestic films and eight foreign films for re-examination. The report lists *Hanyŏ*, along with the Korean films *Gobau* (dir. Cho Jŏng-ho, 1959) and *Obalt'an*, and the foreign films *La tempesta*, *L'Amant de Lady*

Chatterley, *La romana* (*Woman of Rome*, dir. Luigi Zampa, 1954), *Le Rouge et le Noir* (*The Red and the Black*, dir. Claude Autant-Lara, 1954), *Blackboard Jungle* (dir. Richard Brooks, 1955), *Les Tricheurs* (*Youthful Sinners*, dir. Marcel Carné, 1958), *J'irai cracher sur vos tombes* (*I Spit on Your Grave*, dir. Michel Gast, 1959) and *Beat Girl* (dir. Edmond T. Gréville, 1960). Of these films, seven were rejected and banned by the four organisations participating in the re-review – the Ministry of Home Affairs, the Ministry of Education, the Ministry of Information and Communications, and the Ministry of Public Information. The seven banned films were *Obalt'an*, *La tempesta*, *L'Amant de Lady Chatterley*, *La romana*, *Le Rouge et le Noir*, *Les Tricheurs* and *J'irai cracher sur vos tombes*.[71] The documents show that Kim Ki-young's *Hanyŏ* was spared. And in fact, Kim's major works before the mid-1970s – *Hanyŏ* (1960), *Goryŏjang* (1963) and *Hwanyŏ* – did not encounter any major censorship issues. Kim Ki-young would mysteriously reflect in a 1984 interview that although his earlier film-making had included social themes, they nevertheless managed to evade censorship:

I made several films of social criticism, but no matter how harsh the content was, not a single cut of the film was censored. But these days [in the 1980s], such works cannot be made, so I feel like I am directing a film that doesn't have a theme.[72]

Amazingly, *Hanyŏ* garnered both industry- and state-sponsored accolades before and after the coup, a curious feat considering the vast ideological gap between the industry's prioritisation of innovation in film art and the authoritarian state's determination to justify its own rule by praising films that promoted their agendas. Just days *before* the coup, on 3 May 1961, *Hanyŏ* had won Best Director and Best Cinematography at the Second Film Art Awards [*Yŏnghwa Yesulsang*], sponsored by an entertainment newspaper company (the *Yŏnye Sinmunsa*) and a film art company (*Yŏnghwa yesulsa*). This award was administered by film critics and journalists, and nominated films had to meet film art criteria set by a panel of nineteen members.[73] A few months *after* the coup, on 28 December 1961, *Hanyŏ* won several awards at the first Korean Outstanding Quality Film Awards [*Hanguk ch'oe usu yŏnghwasang*],[74] which were launched by the MPI under the military government of Park Chung-hee.[75] By all accounts it was a grand affair. The daily newspaper *Tonga Ilbo* reported details of the awards ceremony that was held at the Grand Hall of the premier Chosŏn Hotel, with a cocktail party attended by the Minister of Public Information, foreign dignitaries and domestic guests, as well as many prominent figures from the film industry. The awards were presented by the 1959 winners from each category. *Hanyŏ* swept the awards, winning in the categories of Best Quality Director (Kim Ki-young), Best Quality New Actress (Yi Ŭn-sim), Best Quality Cinematography (Kim Dŏk-jin), Best Quality Art (Park Sŏk-in) and Best Quality Editing (Oh Yŏng-gŭn).

The acclaim enjoyed by *Hanyŏ* both before and after the end of the Second Republic ultimately suggests dual legacies that exist in tension with one another, which in turn stem from the tension that drives the film itself. The film both releases and contains a figure of unruly social disruption, manifested in a symbol of unrestrained feminine sexuality. It peers into the dark heart of moral depravity and in the same breath laughs it off as fever dream that rises at best to cautionary tale. It is a film that encapsulates the utopian chaos of the Second Republic while managing not to offend the close scrutiny of a repressive authoritarian state. More recently still, it has come to serve as an originating locus for South Korea's blossoming film industry at the turn of the twenty-first century, with prominent directors like Bong Joon Ho citing it as an important influence. *Hanyŏ*, it seems, is a dense text. This density will be the subject of the next chapter.

2 Density and Architecture

Let's return to take a closer look at the closing frame of *Hanyŏ*. As we have seen, much of the film's drama takes place within this modern two-storey house – a house that becomes increasingly vexed and fraught. The turmoil crescendos in a double suicide, the iconic scene of Dong-sik dragging the pleading housemaid – her hands clasped around his ankles – back down the staircase as the rat poison does its work. This is followed a few minutes later by the climactic image of the housemaid's dead body sprawled on the staircase, mid-descent. The film's actual ending, the closing frame, occurs after this dramatic death and returns us to the upstairs piano room, which is across the hall from the maid's room and connected by a balcony to where the affair between the housemaid and Dong-sik had taken place. Somehow, we have returned to a scene of middle-class domestic bliss, signalled by the entrance of the very much alive housemaid, who now dutifully serves drinks to the family. Then everyone else leaves the room, apart from Dong-sik, who abruptly turns to the window

Dong-sik turns to the window pointing his finger, breaking the fourth wall

to address the audience. He reveals with a laugh and a wink that the main action of the film had been a hypothetical, cautionary tale inspired by the newspaper article, circumstances to which all men are susceptible. Pointing his finger, he speaks even more directly to the audience – 'This is true for you! And even you, though you are shaking your head.'

Immediately after Dong-sik breaks the proverbial fourth wall, the camera quickly pulls back. Easily missed, in the split second before the fade to closing credits, are several images that suddenly appear on the surface of the dark window of the house. Although they seem to be reflections of real objects and persons, the ontological and diegetical status of these images is uncertain. We are unsure whether, for example, these images are refracted from a position inside the room, or whether they are reflected from outside the house. Perhaps they are representations of imaginary projections that do not exist at all within the diegesis. Curiously, two separate images suggestive of the housemaid suddenly appear simultaneously in the window as the shot pulls back, even though we know that she is neither in the room nor on the other side of the window. Both the housemaid and Dong-sik's wife had left the room and shut the door just prior to his final address to the audience, so we know that these

Images in the window, possibly of the housemaid, with no referent, to the left and right

images are counterfactual. Blurred but clearly discernible, the figure that resembles the housemaid is to Dong-sik's right (standing and facing him) in the frame.

Another similar figure suggestive of the housemaid stands to his left, facing us, her face obscured by the lamp, which, unlike her, *is* an actual object in the room. When the actual housemaid left the room in the final scene, she was wearing black. The image faces us now in a short-sleeved white sweater, like the one the housemaid wore when she first arrived at the Kims' house and caught a rat with her bare hands in the cluttered kitchen, and also when she is first shown to her room and realises it is connected to the piano room by the balcony. The other image suggestive of the housemaid is dressed in the thin white dress she wears when she seduces Dong-sik, and when she brings the children water and the son, believing that it is poisoned, falls down the stairs and dies. These outfits refer to pivotal moments in the narrative that signal the housemaid's primitive instincts, as well as her sexual impulses, before they burgeon into full-blown threats. Thus, even as the closing frame of the film dismisses the threat of unruly sexuality that has been central to the film's plot, it evokes precisely that threat in these ghostly images. Kim superimposes these images not once but twice in the same frame to reassert the housemaid's presence – and, in turn, consciously replicates her as film image. The housemaid's simultaneous presence and absence in this moment presents what Vivian Sobchack calls the 're-presencing' of a past image, here of the 'suddenly there' housemaid.[76] Although these images may seem accidental, they are likely deliberate if we contrast them with an earlier shot that occurs in the transition from fantasy to 'reality' when the camera pulls us back into the piano room from the position of a seated Jŏng-sim. Dong-sik stands, looking out of the window with his back to us, and in the window, we see a reflection of Jŏng-sim reading the newspaper. Unlike the spectral images of the housemaid, here Jŏng-sim's reflected image has a physical referent, which the camera establishes by consciously pulling back to reveal her in the room, aligning Jŏng-sim with her reflection and Dong-sik's

Jŏng-sim's reflection in the window, to the right, with a
clear referent in the room

perspectival line. This quietly sets up the later shot of spectral images
resembling the housemaid as a kind of reverse shot that serves to
make us conscious of the status of bodily reflections in the window as
an indicator of the dense image.

In addition to the figures resembling the housemaid in the
closing scene, the reflection of a large structure looms in the centre
of the frame above Dong-sik. Possibly the camera filming the scene,
it appears to be covered by a tarp as if to protect it from the rain.

Tarp-covered object above Dong-sik's head. A film camera
on the set?

Ae-sun's illogical reappearance

There is more. The camera pulls further back and the shot begins to fade – as Dong-sik opens the window, his daughter, Ae-sun (Yi Yu-ri), abruptly peeks up beside him from under the windowsill and looks directly at the camera, even though we watched her, just moments before, leaving the room with everyone else. Her reappearance is thus illogical, functioning similarly to the spectral housemaid images, rupturing our gaze on the window as it opens, pulling our focus back into the 'real space' of the room in a state of disorientation and essentially drawing attention to the window. And finally, on the

Woman in striped shirt holding clipboard in the corner of frame. Film crew member?

right-hand side of the screen, we see perhaps the strangest image in this already strange sequence. In the very last moment of the film, the image of a woman from the rear, wearing a striped shirt and white hat, flashes briefly in the lower right corner of the shot. A member of the film crew, it seems – and thus, a different kind of working woman is holding a clipboard, on which is attached a storyboard (a final detail that is very difficult to spot).

In addition to all the elements reflected in the window, various lighting sconces and decorative plates adorn the walls of the room, which is stuffed full of furniture, with a sitting area in the foreground next to the piano and a dining set in the background. These closing shots are thus dense images. They pack in almost too many little details, making it difficult for the eye to apprehend all that these shots contain. In creating these shots, Kim Ki-young pursued what he enigmatically described alternately as a 'dense screen' and 'a density [*mildo*] beyond the limitations of images'.[77] His descriptions of this mysterious principle were often difficult to follow, apparently encompassing various aspects of his film-making practice, but essentially it seems to refer to a maximalist aesthetic in which the film's dense *mise en scène* would match the heightened emotional intensity achieved by the melodramatic plot, enlivened by 'the human being, living, moving around'.[78]

Clutter of objects in the room

Furthermore, the dense shots that close the film not only occur in conjunction with the breaking of the fourth wall, but they are also largely coincident with the house's literal fourth wall – that is, the floor-to-ceiling window in which are reflected all the uncanny, confusing images. The house's fourth wall is, in turn, an appropriate surface for inscribing density because it serves as the central conceptual apparatus of the film's social critique. What *Hanyŏ* ultimately explores is not just the affective emergence of the middle class out of the confusions of the Second Republic but also something like a conceptual architecture established to serve as the discursive location of that emergence. If the Second Republic was a conflicted historical moment defined by the tension between utopian possibility and the threat of chaotic entropy, *Hanyŏ*'s house manifests this tension in its dense material form.

Kim Ki-young creates *density* within the *mise en scène* of the house at the centre of the story and in compressed images embodied by architectural features to reflect the psychological impact of the occupants' interactions. The spatial depth established with rhythmic, apparently seamless continuous editing creates a contradictory sense of structural openness (both of class mobility and the modern architecture of the house) that belies the intensifying density of the *mise en scène* and architectural features as outside forces intrude and close in upon the space. Rather than relieving tension, the openness enables and exerts further pressure from the outside. The increasing density registers the unresolved contradictions that consolidate in aesthetic form the contradictions of compressed modernisation.

The construction of this density is related to the film's thematisation of tension discussed in the previous chapter. Density in *Hanyŏ*, I argue, is tension becoming concretised into a conceptual formation, figured by the house, which itself becomes the object of attention and thereby dissipates any urgency to address the persistent tensions. But since those tensions persist even as we are less bothered by them – indeed, they are built into the architecture of the house – the density that Kim builds into his images disturbs us in uncanny registers, reminding us that historical struggle was repressed rather than resolved. Politically speaking, we can think of the house in *Hanyŏ* as anticipating the ideological bargain that allowed the authoritarian government of Park Chung-hee to stabilise social and economic policy, creating conditions for rapid economic growth during the 1960s at the cost of deferring, often with violent measures, the promise of democracy in South Korea indefinitely. More concretely, in *Hanyŏ*, the house is the object of a nascent middle-class desire, from which unruly disturbances must be expelled without addressing what gave rise to them in the first place.

Architectural desire

Featuring many of the period's status symbols, the house in *Hanyŏ* is two storeys tall, built in a modern, western style, and stands on its own property surrounded by a stone wall. It has floor-to-ceiling windows and a balcony that wraps around the front of the entire upper floor, showcasing the piano room and the housemaid's room, which are connected by additional windows that overlook the stairway landing. For both the Kims and the housemaid, the move to the house is a new encounter with modern architecture. While waiting for the house to be completed, the family has been living in small, cramped accommodation on the property, and the

A view of the house from the outside

The housemaid arrives at the Kims' new house and finds
the kitchen

housemaid's home is the factory dormitory (as mentioned earlier, she
initially emerges, in fact, from a closet). At first, the move into the
main house seems to anticipate the 'my sweet home' or 'my home
[*maihom*]' discourse that appeared in Korean popular media later
in the 1960s,[79] and even then as 'an aspirational term rather than a
descriptive one',[80] and still a fantasy.[81] As quickly becomes apparent,
though, this ideal site of middle-class emergence becomes more like
the haunted house of horror films, a socio-psychological space that
entraps rather than enables its inhabitants.[82] Appropriately, the
external shots of the house are most often shrouded in darkness and
stormy weather.

Initially coming from a theatrical background, Kim Ki-young
was well known for his preference for shooting on film sets rather
than on location. The house in *Hanyŏ* is often described as
resembling an indoor theatrical stage. He preferred shooting on
sets because it afforded him more control and, as he described,
the 'freedom and opportunity to concentrate'.[83] The shooting
of *Hanyŏ* took about two months, a month longer than was
standard at the time, and the film's production consisted of shooting
approximately five hundred scenes, which take place predominantly
within the house.[84]

The architectural features of the house are designed to support dramatic narrative development and complement filmic composition, rather than facilitate practical living. For instance, in reality a housemaid would not have occupied an upstairs bedroom away from the kitchen and entrance; but sharing the upper floor with Dongsik's piano room enabled the tracking shots of their movements as they go back and forth across the balcony. It also allowed Kim Ki-young to show both rooms in a single frame, a juxtaposition in which the housemaid's bedroom functions as a threatening contrast to the living room as the site of blissful domesticity. In addition, the layout of the house serves to structurally organise an allegory of social ascent and descent through its emphasis on the staircase and becomes cinematically inscribed with the changing psychological state of the characters as they transgress moral and social interdicts. In so doing, the layout exhibits the film's fascination with conflating the characters' bodies with the architecture, the clutter of objects, and an obstinate interest in windows and frames. The film's slow boil of intrigue and voyeurism involves the repeated opening and closing of sliding doors and windows, and the characters are constantly entering and leaving rooms. As if incorporating their bodies into the architectural features, the characters are also consistently depicted as pressed up against the windows or wedged between the sliding doors.

The housemaid pressed up against the window

The housemaid holding a glass of water and seeing the staircase through it. Poisoned or not?

The house's stairs are one prominent site in the film where social psychology is rendered in relation to built architecture. They are a site of not just ascension and descension in a metaphorics that registers class but also one of conflict and violence suggesting the means through which class change is effected. The kitchen is on the ground floor at the bottom of the stairs, so the housemaid makes frequent use of the stairs when bringing food and drinks upstairs. She mediates our view of the staircase. For instance, when she carries the glass of water upstairs pretending it is poisoned, the distorted stairs are visible through the water in a close-up shot of her hand holding the glass. Two main plot events also happen on the staircase.

The first is the killing of Dong-sik's son (An Sŏng-gi) when the housemaid pushes him down the stairs. The housemaid brings him a glass of water and tells him there was rat poison in it after he drinks it. 'You're going to die! Go tell your father.' She pushes the gasping Ch'ang-sun through the door and he tumbles down the stairs crying for Dong-sik. This is a moment in the story when the power dynamic between the housemaid and Dong-sik shifts. The son's fall is swift, captured by a cut from a split second at the top of the stairs to a shot from the bottom, as we see him roll down the steps. Dong-sik and Jŏng-sim come out of their bedroom, and as they crouch over their

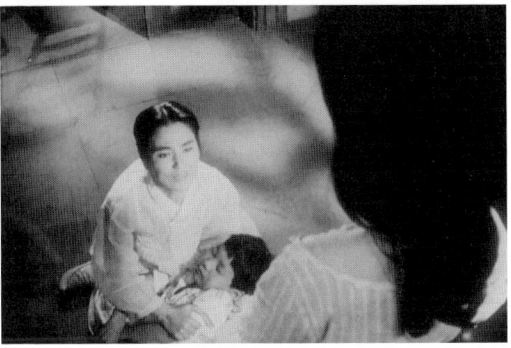

The son falls to his death; the power dynamic shifts

son's body, Dong-sik turns his gaze to the top of the stairs. Shot from a low angle, he rushes up to grab the housemaid, who resists Dong-sik's attempt to drag her downstairs, as Jŏng-sim kneels by her dead child at the bottom and looks up. A struggle ensues between Dong-sik and the housemaid at the top of the stairs under the light of the wall lamp as he violently tries to strangle her, and a high angle is sustained by keeping visible just in the left corner a sliver of the lit, empty family room downstairs, creating a diagonal line. The housemaid recalls here the death of her own child, which Jŏng-sim had forced her to miscarry by falling down the stairs. Ch'ang-sun died because he believed the water was poisoned, and when Ae-sun asks her why she lied, the housemaid tells the family that it is something she learned from the children's parents. Registering the fact that the maid has gained the upper hand in the power struggle, the perspective has shifted, now to a sharp high angle, with the back of the housemaid's head in looming and dark contrast to the wife's small figure clad in white.

The second event is the slow death of the housemaid on those same stairs as she is dragged down one step at a time. Shot from a low angle from the bottom of the stairs, the maid is seen holding on to Dong-sik's leg as her body is dragged down towards the bottom of the staircase, her head looking up to the ceiling. Alternating between close-up shots of his delirious face and her head slowly hitting each step as she screams, their descent, although physically entwined, occurs distinctly, connected through editing. The camera pulls back to show them in the same frame again once they have reached the bottom of the stairs and he breaks away from her grip as she reaches for him and dies. In this scene, our perspective becomes fragmented, as the shots of Dong-sik show him focused straight ahead, while the shots of the housemaid show her looking up as she descends. The weight of her head accentuates each step of the stairs, and when she releases her hold just before dying, she reaches out her arms towards the camera in a final desperate cry. The incorporation of her body into the staircase, arms and legs extended into the steps,

The housemaid loses her death grip on Dong-sik's leg

emphasises the verticality of the staircase. As the camera pulls back, the sound of the baby is the last sound we hear before the narrative cuts to the final window-framing device. The baby's crying recalls the danger posed by the staircase to children as it becomes inscribed with the fall of their crippled daughter, the death of their son, the forced miscarriage of the housemaid's unborn child and, in this final moment, the wailing cry of the Kims' newborn child overlaid onto the shot. When the camera then pulls away from the far back of Jŏng-sim's workroom, where she crouches over Dong-sik's dead body, the shot is aligned with her view of the dead housemaid on the stairs. The central narrative concludes here with a shot similar to the film's beginning, when we first visited the new house, in which the camera pulled back to create a deep field of vision and we watched Ae-sun fall down the stairs, establishing the dangerous verticality of the staircase. This time, it is inscribed with the housemaid's immobile body incorporated into the architecture of the house.

Thus, the staircase becomes a site of quickly shifting fortunes and dispossession ensuing from learned behaviour, and such scenes on the stairs accrue in density as each one recalls another. We are reminded that the housemaid's violent struggle with Dong-sik is also a repetition of the scene of his assault of Kyŏng-hŭi on the stairs when she had threatened to falsely accuse him of rape, except that the outcome of the housemaid learning to seduce Dong-sik by watching them in that scene is now very different. The events on the staircase force the characters to establish unexpected moral and social parameters. In the first murder scene involving the staircase, Dong-sik is compelled to do as the housemaid bids, as Jŏng-sim fears how others will perceive them, and how it may affect their jobs. Jŏng-sim's response is startling in its dissonance with the expected response of a mother to the death of her child. In the second murder scene in which death occurs on the staircase, the tables are turned as the violence done to the housemaid serves as recompense for the damage she has inflicted on the household; and the invocation of violence done to children in the scene, including the housemaid's unborn child, suggests the radically destructive consequences of her ambitions, an irony to be sure, since we have seen how these ambitions are modelled on normative middle-class dreams. Thus, the staircase also becomes a site at which characters clash in their efforts to achieve their aspirations, imperilling the very forms of social and biological reproduction that the middle-class home is otherwise supposed to secure.

Importantly, the film foregrounds the actual construction of the house. When Kyŏng-hŭi comes to ask for piano lessons, Dong-sik takes her on a tour of the then unfinished house, still in the early stages of construction. Our first view of the house begins inside, where the camera is positioned on the ground floor. We view the scene from the centre of the main hallway at the bottom of the staircase. Wooden beams lean scattered against the wall, and Dong-sik's daughter, on crutches, comes looking for her brother, who sits on the stairs and taunts her. As Dong-sik and Kyŏng-hŭi enter, the camera pulls back to reveal the space behind it, showing the downstairs sitting room that will double as the wife's sewing space. Pulling back the camera, a technique that Kim uses throughout the film, has the effect of extending space, and in turn creating depth in our field of vision. Dong-sik tells Kyŏng-hŭi that the house will be laid with linoleum floors as they walk on the ground floor through the living room to the bedroom off to the left, and Kyŏng-hŭi pauses

A tour of the new house still under construction

in the door frame. She will cross this threshold later when she introduces the housemaid to the house.

The camera setup is optimally positioned here to show us the entrance, the staircase – on which the characters will variously climb, descend or die – and the doorways to Dong-sik and Jŏng-sim's bedroom to the left and kitchen to the right. The layout of the set accommodates this revealing camera angle, offering up the house as an inward-looking space of interior depth, a house in which the physical is inseparable from the psychological. In this context, this opening tour of the house suggests not just the connection between its physical layout and the characters that will later inhabit it but also the construction of that spatialised psychology. Indeed, this is the origin point of Kyŏng-hŭi's desire for Dong-sik (and the life in that house that a relationship with him would entail) and of the housemaid's desire, which is modelled, as we have seen, on Kyŏng-hŭi's. We also might think of this tour of the newly built middle-class home more broadly as a nascent vision of the Korean middle class, not yet fully formed by this point in 1960.

Window walls

The construction of this middle-class desire, structured in architectural terms, is in turn complemented by the film's preoccupation with windows, and their implication of voyeurism. The house has more than the average number of tall, panelled windows for houses of its era. We are turned into voyeurs throughout the film, looking in through these many windows from unidentified positions outside the house. Unlike Hitchcock's *Rear Window* (1954), in which the spectator follows Jimmy Stewart's intrusive camera and binocular-aided gaze as he spies on his neighbours across the courtyard, the gaze is not that of a specific character in *Hanyŏ*. Furthermore, as viewers, we are not often at a remove, instead watching through more immersive tight shots, even when our view is from outside of the house. We experience the house for the most part as a series of tightly framed fragments; and our first full view

Light in the upstairs piano room

of the entire house does not occur until thirty-seven minutes into the film, in the scene preceding Kyŏng-hŭi's confession of her love. In this scene, Dong-sik and Kyŏng-hŭi return from the funeral of Sŏn-yŏng, the factory girl who loses her job and returns home after Dong-sik reports her for harassment. It is evening, the house stands on the left half of the frame at an angle, lit up inside the wall that runs diagonally along the bottom of the frame. The right half of the frame is pitch-dark. Lightning strikes ominously as they approach the gate in a car; we then cut to the piano room, where the housemaid is playing the piano, although Dong-sik had forbidden her to do so. Up until this point, we have only seen aspects of the interior of the house, from its construction to completion, scaling the outside walls and windows for glimpses in but without any establishing long shots of the building. But even this view of the house exterior positions our gaze simultaneously in the interiority of the car from afar, in effect linking one interior of modernity (the car) to another (the house).

Frequently, the shot is so close to the house it is unclear if we are viewing the scene from inside or from outside through a window. When the housemaid seduces Dong-sik, after Kyŏng-hŭi's failed attempt, a long tracking shot follows them as they cross from the piano room to the housemaid's room along the balcony. The camera alternates from a position inside, then outside, the window.

Tracking shot from the piano room to the housemaid's room along the balcony

The housemaid undresses in the room while looking outside, and as she moves to slide the window closed, we realise that it had been open the whole time and that we had not been looking through it as first presumed. It is only through the characters' actions that we can tell if the window is there at all. Kim Ki-young makes prominent use of similar shots involving windows throughout *Hanyŏ*. Sometimes we are made aware that we are witnessing action inside the house through a window. Other times, we are unaware that we are looking through a window; and in still other moments, we are mistaken in believing that a window is there when actually it is open. This kind of window play makes us aware of the fact of mediation even as we are uncertain about its operations.

This uncertainty regarding the function of the film's windows becomes even more significant at the end when the fourth wall, which is of course a window in this case, is broken. Here, we should return to the reflection of the large object shrouded in what appears to be a wet tarp looming in the centre of the window. We can speculate that this object (not visible elsewhere in the film) is the camera shooting the scene; and given Kim's reputation for meticulous and seamless editing – especially with his window shots in this film – we may infer that it is intended to be seen. Combined with the brief shot of the woman who seems to be a member of the film crew, we appreciate how the ending of the film self-reflexively links the voyeurism it has thematised throughout in relation to unruly sexuality here to film apparatus. It now juxtaposes the uncanny images of the housemaid in the window in the final moments of the film to what seems to be a shot of the camera, via a reflection in the same window, pointed back at the audience.

This final scene thus synthesises film as moving image with the structural and material features of modern architecture. Film and architecture interact self-reflexively to produce, and not just give representation to, a relationship between the built environment and our internal lives. Design thus has implications for human subjectivity, offering what Anne Friedberg has described as 'a frame for perspectival view' that we observe in both architecture and film.[85] Lamenting the primordial idea of the house as 'a shelter, an enclosed space, which affords protection against cold, heat *and outside observation*', the architect Le Corbusier referred to the window as an '*organ* of the house', alluding to its function as comparable to the eye.[86] With the development of new building technologies in the early twentieth century, walls no longer had to be load-bearing and big extended glass windows were possible. The window of a modern house thus 'fulfills its true destiny' as a 'provider of light' and as 'walls of light'[87] that both let air through and are able to be looked through, functioning essentially, as Beatriz Colomina points out, like 'images as walls' – that is, a '(movie) screen'.[88]

The uncanny images of the housemaid in the window in the final shot of *Hanyŏ* enact, then, what Anthony Vidler saw as early cinema's ability to '"construct" its own architecture in light and shade, scale and movement', allowing for 'a mutual intersection of these two "spatial arts"'. Film enabled architecture to 'play', while architecture afforded filmic art with 'the potential to develop a new architecture of time and space unfettered by the material constraints of gravity and daily life'.[89] The depth of Kim Ki-young's window contrasts with the absence of a correlating reference point, severing the images from any kind of logical relationship between interiority

Window walls

and exteriority. Displaced onto the window, and visible all at once, are the images of the housemaid extracted from what has already happened in the film, located in between the 'inside' and 'outside'.

In this context, Dong-sik breaking, reinstating, opening and rupturing the fourth wall/window in *Hanyŏ* becomes a way to enable conscious recognition of how and what we see. But it is unclear whether breaking the fourth wall in a direct address of the audience functions, ultimately, to 'open' the film. Indeed, revealing in the final shot the closed window immediately after breaking the fourth wall would seem to counter any move towards openness. That the proverbial fourth wall here is, of course, not a wall but a window further complicates the matter. Is this a permeable barrier or ultimately a limit? Dong-sik breaks the fourth wall but only to reimpose the film's ultimately conservative impulse – the containment of feminine threat. The fact that we see, however, the images of the housemaid in the window – and that we see her through the window throughout the film, pressing against the window and passing in and out of windows as if they were doors – suggests that despite Dong-sik's attempts to refuse that which enters the house, the fourth wall is permeable in both directions. By signalling the permeability of the fourth wall, and thus refuting any boundary or foreclosure of the social from the representational world of the home, the images of the housemaid in the window, severed from logical referents inside or outside the house, index the contradiction at the heart of the film: that the housemaid must be disavowed because she embodies precisely the same aspirations of the upwardly mobile middle-class family that lives in the house. She only threatens the household because she herself so desperately wants to occupy it.

Image density

As epitomised by the myriad of elements that compose the final shots of the film, the pursuit of density was central to Kim Ki-young's film aesthetic in *Hanyŏ*. This pursuit began with set design; the design of the house – built entirely on a sound stage to Kim's precise specifications – drew on conventions of the theatre to create compressed spaces with dizzying perspectival contours. It is important that we first enter the house before it is completed and before its rooms become adorned with furniture and wall dressings. These initial shots emphasise the vertical and horizonal lines that compose the house's framing, establishing a grid that remains a visual leitmotif throughout the film.[90]

In our first sight of the house after the Kims have moved in, we see just Dong-sik, tuning the piano in his room, in a shot from a camera positioned outside the window. The dark window frames invoke this grid, bisecting the film frame into multiple vertical panels, each panel seemingly separate, crammed with their own elements, leaving little empty space. The shot of the bisected window then transitions into the room and to the door frame as Dong-sik's son and then Kyŏng-hŭi enter. The frame-to-frame transition, and the split-screen effect achieved not through special editing but rather through the house's architectural features (its windows), function to distort clear spatial divisions. The sliding doors and windows allow for a modularity of shifting panels that disorients. These visual elements draw attention to how we, unconsciously, seek to create a visual whole – assembling the images within the various window panels, bisected by the wooden frames, to constitute a single image – to spatially orient ourselves.

Vertical window/door framing: Dong-sik tunes the piano; Kyŏng-hŭi enters through the door

This visual gridding in relation to the house's architecture is then filled with interior design – material touches and objects are crammed into each room and hung on the walls. The couple's primary bedroom, for example, features a large bed with a headboard consisting of wooden posts fixed at right angles that invoke the house's architectural framing. The vertical lines of the headboard are in turn matched by the folds of the curtain that decorates the wall at the head of the bed, over which are hung a series of images mounted in rectangular frames. The perpendicular wall is wood-panelled but relatively bare by comparison, decorated with another framed image and a lighting sconce above it. The visual grid formed by the

The happy couple against their vertical wooden bedframe

vertical and horizontal lines in the shot is then further complicated
by the chiaroscuro lighting, which is used throughout the film in
other rooms to produce a similar effect.[91] All this gridding works to
subdivide the larger framework of the house into smaller and tighter
increments. In the corner of the room is a large dresser, on top of
which are several ornamental objects, including some books, a pair
of vases and a creepy-looking doll in a black dress – a figure evoking
the housemaid herself, who wears a black dress in the film's climactic
scene – overlooking the couple as they lie in bed. The other rooms of
the house are similarly cluttered with odd objects, including masks
that occupy various nooks, positioned in corners and hung high on
walls, as if watching the drama occurring in the rooms they garnish.

The packed house, full of strange tchotchkes that serve
as uncanny totems for repressed tension, is magnified by Kim's
promiscuous approach to genre. As the director himself revealed,
the film at its core has a 'very melodramatic structure', but he also
mobilises a variety of influences – notably German Expressionism,
Surrealism, Modernism, film noir, horror, the grotesque and elements
of the Gothic, as previously mentioned – grafting this disparate
array onto the film's melodramatic core while stripping it of the
genre's characteristic sentimentalism.[92] By some accounts, *Hanyŏ*,
in turn, gave rise to the modern Korean horror genre with the figure

of the ghostly and monstrous housemaid and in its development of murder, torture and sexual perversity;[93] and it was perhaps Kim's proclivity for this kind of generic grafting that allowed the emergence of this new genre years later. He was often asked about the various 'isms' attributed to his distinct style but enigmatically refuted such categorisations as the task of film critics, confirming only his committed interest in the psychological, and specifically in the psychoanalytic theories of Freud, germinating in *Hanyŏ*.

In addition to density in *mise en scène* and genre, Kim Ki-young also produced density in his camerawork and intricate editing practices in *Hanyŏ*. Kim had carefully studied Hitchcock's long takes and realised that in many cases several cameras had been used in a meticulously planned series of shots and skilfully connected to produce the effect of seamless continuity, as if the scene was one long take taken with one camera.[94] In addition, Kim was inspired by Hitchcock's so-called 'ten-minute take' as featured, for example, in *Rope* (1948). In *Hanyŏ*, Kim's exactitude in cutting and near undetectable continuous editing enabled him to maintain 'high density' in his long takes, without making audiences overtly conscious of the camera, which he saw as the disadvantage of the technique. Along with a copious use of tracking shots that enabled him to follow transgressions across spaces in the house, and frequent pulling of the camera in and out to establish dimensions, these techniques facilitated a greater depth of field in his shots and add layers to the images of psychological torment and angst. Thus, it is the work of the camera, as much as the plot, that gives us a glimpse into the unconscious desires and sexual urges of Korea's modernity.

In *Hanyŏ*, all of these elements pertaining to *mise en scène*, genre and editing combine to produce what David Bordwell calls 'long-term density', a reference to the simultaneous density of the built environment, of the psychology of the characters and of the filmic composition. Bordwell's concept is achieved diachronically both in the narrative as well as in audience memory through the way an object or prop is placed or used, such that 'one scene recalls another not only by similarity of situation and locale but by tangible marks left on it by earlier action'. It primes us to 'recall earlier action in the locale', and as characters leave their 'marks and spoors in the space, and those get activated as memories … the settings can bear the impress of human transit, leading us to recall bits of behavior and emotional states'.[95] As we have seen, the staircase and the windows at the top of the staircase (which extend on each side to the windows of the piano room and the housemaid's room) are key features of the house, registering the ascent, descent and transgressions of the people inside. In addition, pictorial density and depth of composition – what Bordwell calls 'scenic density' – is achieved by using up the entirety of the space within the frame. The result is 'snug compositions' with salient elements that work like 'a field of dynamic masses', objects and emotions alike that are easily entangled and activated.[96] In this manner, *Hanyŏ* produces a densely rich affective sensorium that preserves the tensions that animated a complicated transitional moment in South Korean history.

This density also anticipates the rapid socio-economic transition that will occur later that decade, which Chang Kyung-sup famously described as 'compressed modernity'. Indeed, we can think of density as the consequence of the physics of compression. The concept has been particularly influential for describing modern Korean history because it pertains not just to economic transition but also to 'various levels of human existence and experience – that is, personhood, family, secondary organizations, urban/rural localities, societal units (including civil society and nation), and, not least importantly, the global society'.[97] Perhaps most significantly then, compressed modernity destabilises daily life for ordinary people, requiring intense, intricate and flexible management (according to Chang) to address this upheaval. In addition to representing the threat to middle-class stability, the housemaid also signifies the kind of broader social turmoil that Chang references. And if *Hanyŏ*'s density requires management, as is examined in the next chapter, it does so by attempting to organise and create frisson in the attention of the audience.

3 Frisson

On several occasions, Kim Ki-young liked to share an anecdote about the audience's experience watching *Hanyŏ*. Women were so engrossed by the housemaid's seduction of Dong-sik, he explained, that on multiple occasions they stood up in the theatre, shouting 'Kill that bitch!'[98] This story is frequently mentioned in the discourse of *Hanyŏ*'s popular reception. It provides a useful opening for our enquiry here into how the film caught spectators off guard, confronting them with their own process of viewing. *Hanyŏ* called attention to the very act of cinematic viewing itself, as well as the ambivalences built into watching a film; the reaction of the women in the theatre epitomises these ambivalences, expressing equal parts thrill and agitation. Inhering in the ambivalence of watching, in turn, was an emerging compressed aesthetics itself, reflective of the logic of industrialisation, which compelled modes of reception responsive to the film's subversion of social mores and thus expressed the uncertainties triggered by the acceleration, fragmentation and condensation of compressed modernisation.

The famous scene that prompted such a strong reaction from women in the theatrical audience consists of several close-up shots of about three seconds each. It comprises a sequence of different parts of the maid's body after she removes the top of her wet dress: Dong-sik's hand by her breasts held under her arm, her bare feet standing on his shoes and her hands clasped around his back. All are crosscut with close-ups of Dong-sik's face, and his increasingly anguished desire when confronted by her determined seduction. A storm rages outside and lightning pierces the night; the scene cuts to a shot of a tree outside the walls of the house. Immediately, the tree is struck by lightning and bursts into thick smoke; the camera retreats into darkness. The scene then cuts to the factory music room where

Seduction; lightning strikes the tree outside the wall of the house; music lesson in the factory music room: 'Away with the murderer!'

a woman is writing 'Away with the murderer!' on a chalkboard. She is mobilising the factory women against Dong-sik for his role in Sŏn-yŏng's death. The cuts seem to proceed from a scene of action to a scene of reaction, and they jump from a voyeur's perspective, watching the seduction from outside the house, to an immersed audience perspective, as we become part of a collective gathered around a scene unfolding within the diegesis, partaking in a shared sense of moral outrage.

Positioned in between the seduction scene and the mobilisation scene, the image of the lightning-struck tree going up in smoke functions like Sergei Eisenstein's description of the image of the wave smashing into the pier at the beginning of *Bronenosets Potyomkin* (*Battleship Potemkin*, 1925) – what he called an 'ecstatic explosion'. For Eisenstein, the smashing wave prefaced and condensed the focus of the whole film, functioning both as a 'symbol of violent unrest' and a 'kinesthetic prompt for the audience'.[99] In *Hanyŏ*, the smoking tree is both a symbol of the psychological impact of compressed modernisation (and the irrepressible desires bound up with it), as well as a prompt that encourages the audience to react emotionally to what they have just witnessed – just as the female audience did, yelling at the screen. This fragmented sequence – the scene of Dong-sik's affair with the maid, the burning tree and the music room incitement – does not come to anything. The factory women are judging Dong-sik here not for his affair with the maid (about which they are unaware) but for the death of the factory worker, Sŏn-yŏng, after Dong-sik reports her for harassment and she is fired. Their anger is ironic, since in Sŏn-yŏng's case, Dong-sik has upheld his marriage by rejecting her advances. But because it is placed directly after the scene of his affair with the housemaid, their reaction seems justified. The reaction of the factory women aligns with that of the audience to the transgression we have just witnessed.

The shot of the lightning strike on the tree is also one of a few moments in the film that utilises the other technique Eisenstein perfected: montage. Although not a dominant feature, Kim Ki-young intersperses montage elements at key moments in the film, including the funeral scene and the bar scene. If the ecstatic explosion of the lightning strike seizes the audience's attention, these moments of montage function to reframe the narrative within a broader social context, connecting what is literally depicted in the film to a larger category of experience – social responsibility, in the case of the funeral scene, and urban modernity in the case of the bar scene. Not coincidentally, both montage scenes take place outside the confines of the home. If the house connotes the intensification of interpersonal conflict in a claustrophobic *mise en scène*, then these moments of montage in external locations link the relevance of what happens inside the walls of the house to the societal structures outside. Kim's striking use of montage creates a juxtaposition of images that seems to anticipate compressed modernisation's jarring effect on Korean society. His selection and combination of shots in montage was attentive to cinema's capacity to actively engage the spectator, in Eisenstein's terms, by 'arranging images in the feelings and mind of the spectator' – what he described as the spectator 'being drawn into the process as it occurs'.[100]

Hanyŏ mediated underlying anxieties about contemporary social change, particularly those relating to psychic conflict, and in so doing, registered a deterioration in existing norms of narrative and clarity in visual representation. The film deployed strategies drawn from the logic of rapid industrialisation – fragmentation, acceleration, distortion and obfuscation – that drew attention to the formation of visual knowledge that prefigured what I call a *compressed aesthetics* that would go on to become representative of compressed modernity. On one level, *Hanyŏ* built *tension*, among other elements, between fantasy and reality to emphasise the increasingly pressurised plot, a pressure which in turn also captured the uncertainties of the Second Republic, when utopian promise was balanced against a sense of foreboding danger. On another level, Kim Ki-young created *density* within the house's architecture and in the film's aesthetics more broadly to reflect the psychological impact of the changing world that the house represented, a world that would come to be described as Korea's compressed modernity. *Hanyŏ*'s density was a means to anticipate the rapid formation of a new modern social order that would emerge in the 1960s, coalescing around an emergent middle class, and to register the unresolved contradictions that congealed into those social formations and that have threatened to periodically re-emerge ever since. Tension in narrative structure and density in images characterise compressed aesthetics.

The tension and density built into *Hanyŏ* created *frisson* in its reception. This is an ambivalent affective state that implies delight and thrill on one hand but can also include shock and horror on the other. By inspiring the frisson of his audience, Kim Ki-young in turn pushed them to reflect at the same time on an emerging understanding of psychological conflict specific to compressed modernisation, creating expressions of frisson in the relationships between images and scenes, thereby subverting a clear visuality and redirecting viewers to question existing modes of perception. As a rejoinder to the kind of density described in Chapter 2 – in which the historical tensions of the period become concretised, even while deferring the actual work of resolution – *Hanyŏ*'s use of *frisson* reveals its attempt to organise perception and enable us to see what had previously been invisible; in short, *Hanyŏ* makes audiences conscious of the socio-historical processes with which we are unwittingly engaged while also redefining how we see these processes.

Distortion and disorientation

As the anecdote at the beginning of this chapter suggests, the housemaid was a crucial and effective element in orienting viewers' responses to a compressed aesthetics of distorted and disorienting images. But crucially, they were invited to take pleasure in their own disorientation, to experience *frisson*. In *Hanyŏ*, the housemaid functions like a decoding device, alerting viewers to what Christian Suhr and Rane Willerslev call a 'transcultural montage', in which different elements of a transcultural range of artistic and cultural influences constitute more than just the sum of different components. In the transcultural montage, montage amplifies invisibility and generates space for 'the opening of a gap or fissure, through which the invisible emerges'.[101] So much was not yet visible in South Korea in 1960. As we have seen, this was a moment of rapid transition and great uncertainty; ideas like democracy and the middle class were on the horizon, but not yet realised. Amid this propulsive push into the unknown, *Hanyŏ* attempted to make visible (and pleasurable) the subconscious fantasies that undergirded such promises and, perhaps even more importantly, the struggles that achieving them might entail.

The housemaid herself embodies this kind of emerging visibility. Within the world of *Hanyŏ* created by such transcultural montage, the housemaid's body fills in the gaps and fissures amid the inundation of visual images, media and objects, and provides a focal point. She establishes perspectival lines when there are multiple perspectives and temporalities, and draws attention to conventional, normative modes of perception as they are redrawn, here determined by the intervening role of the cinematic apparatus and the perception this enables. We see glimpses of her on three separate occasions in the factory early in the film, before we are introduced to her within the plot. In each case, she appears – always cleaning – during a short transitional scene that cuts immediately to another location.

At the beginning of the film, after the cut to the factory, we see the two factory women (Kyŏng-hŭi and Sŏn-yŏng) framed in the gaps of the large mechanical spools spinning the textiles. When the machinery comes to a halt, the film cuts to our first view of the housemaid, who emerges from the camera position in the centre of the frame with her back to us pushing a mop straight up the line of the hallway in the middle of the image, into the crowd of approaching factory women. At the end of the hallway, she turns to the right; the camera also tracks right, following the approaching women moving in the same direction into a locker room to the right of the screen. The housemaid disappears from our view as the scene moves into the locker room. Here the housemaid is literally visible but does not

The housemaid hides in plain sight: the first and second time we see her

yet draw our attention other than the fact that the movement of her body carries our line of vision as it transitions; she is just part of the background that we take for granted. But as such, she functions also to embody the fact that although we are watching events unfolding on screen, there are things we are more inclined to see and follow (such as the letter as it switches hands) and things that we do not *see* (such as the maid in the periphery), and that part of our inability to see is a result of how we see and perceive visual images. In the second of her three appearances, we see Sŏn-yŏng running up the stairs towards the dormitory after her suspension. The housemaid is there on the side of the stairs mopping, and the scene cuts to a shot of her feet and mop as

Mopping the stairs as Sŏn-yŏng runs by

Sŏn-yŏng scurries by. This brief shot foreshadows the association of the housemaid with the stairs. Our third view of the housemaid before we become attentive to her at all is another shot of her mopping the same hallway. This time, she appears from the left of the frame and moves down the hallway, passing Dong-sik as he emerges from the music room on the left and the women from the locker room on the right. The long stick of the mop creates lines with its shadow, and as the housemaid pushes the mop, she follows this shadow into the crowd converging in the hallway. This time, she has crossed paths with Dong-sik. In all these cases, the housemaid hides in plain sight.

The third time we see the housemaid, passing by Dong-sik

By establishing an understanding of non-representational images as representing psychological states, the scene in which Dong-sik tries to strangle the housemaid (the second time) is telling. The distorted image is mediated through the housemaid's body, which amplifies a disorienting effect. Compared to the scene in which Dong-sik tries to strangle Kyŏng-hŭi at the top of the stairs, in which a clear and focused image is sustained, the attempt to strangle the housemaid after she stabs Kyŏng-hŭi with a knife is shot in a sustained, distorted close-up of an object on the wall that is in the housemaid's line of vision. As she averts her eyes from Dong-sik's face, the white bust mounted on the wall goes in and out of focus and morphs. The frisson struck between our clear view of the strangling and the housemaid's blurred vision impacted by her loss of consciousness in the face of the attack establishes a synthesising relation between the visible action and the invisible psychological toll as she gasps for breath. In the context of the scene, this distorted image corresponds with Dong-sik's strained face as he tries to kill the housemaid, and clear close-ups of his face precede and follow the distortion, creating a contrast. The distorted image, to which we are directed by the housemaid, renders clear visuality inadequate in representing Dong-sik's vexation as he struggles.

This contrast of clear and distorted images to guide audiences in reading the visualisation of psychological states seemed to be effective. An extensive review of *Hanyŏ* published in the film journal *Kukje Yŏnghwa* in March 1961 suggested that while 'the return to reality at the end [of the film] felt passive', 'it might have been a necessary condition in order to relieve the audience's fatigue'.[102] *Hanyŏ*'s strategy of bringing together heterogeneous elements and clear as well as distorted images was demanding and thus tiring for audiences, the review suggests. Furthermore, it acknowledges Kim Ki-young's exceptional editing skills, and is attentive to what it sees as a 'theory of emotions' [*kamjŏngron*][103] that emerges from the film's psychological elements and the performance of the actors. What resonated with audiences was the heightened emotional delivery of

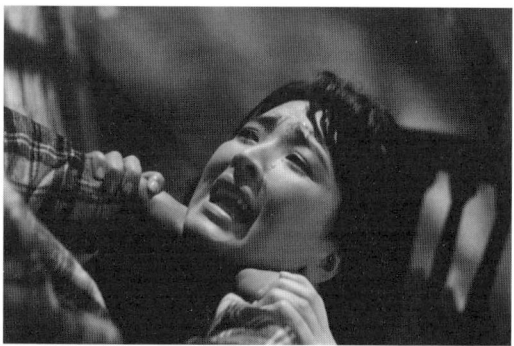

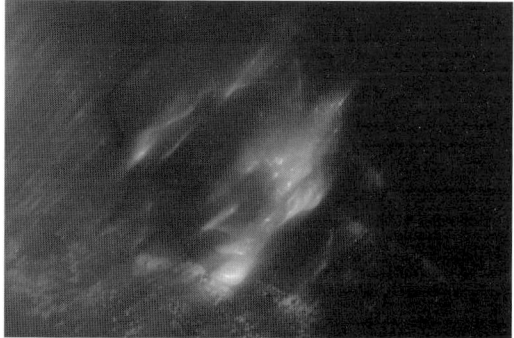

The housemaid looks at the bust as she is strangled; the
housemaid's vision gets distorted; Dong-sik's strained face

the actors in giving voice and corporeal movement to 'psychologically abnormal persons' [*isang simnija*],[104] but the review also explored how the elements of the performance – namely, acting – were implicit choices that existed in an interactive relationship with the cinematic elements – such as editing. Ultimately, this tangled relationship echoed Cynthia Baron's suggestion that in film-making, 'choices about framing, editing, production, and sound design can actually be seen as implicit choices about performance, and acting choices can be seen as implicit choices about other cinematic strategies'.[105]

Montage compression

If the *frisson* inspired by the film allowed audiences to thrill in spectacles of moral depravity, montage for Kim Ki-young became a useful cinematic tool for expressing the ambivalence of this affect. According to David Bordwell, in the Soviet film tradition, montage 'was used to build a narrative (by formulating an artificial time and space or guiding the viewer's attention from one narrative point to another), to control rhythm, to create metaphors, and to make rhetorical points'.[106] Kim used montage in this sense to manage the film's deployment of contradictory states of experience, the foremost of which is modernity itself, which offers new pleasures (the comforts of a new house) but is accompanied by a new set of unanticipated horrors. Jŏng-sim's dream of dying rats might serve as a brief example of Kim's montage, and there are other moments (like the lightning strike) that are evocative of the technique, but I will focus here on the two most obvious sequences of montage in *Hanyŏ*: the scene of Sŏn-yŏng's funeral and the bar scene. In these scenes, both of which, importantly, take place outside the house, montage functions, I would argue, to connect what has been a contained story about domestic conflict to the world beyond the walls of the house. Highly stylised and more visually ostentatious than most of the film, these montage scenes imply the relevance of the domestic story to the broader world from which it emerges, and ultimately its relevance to the emergent modernity of this moment in Korean history.

The funeral montage begins immediately after a scene in which the news of Sŏn-yŏng's death interrupts a music lesson at the factory; Dong-sik had been joking with the factory women about his weekend at his wife's family orchard, when someone rushes in and shares the news, shocking the women. The ensuing montage consists of four shots. In the first, Dong-sik and Kyŏng-hŭi walk along the hallway to the overseer's office, in a long shot that zooms in closer. The scene quickly cuts to a close shot of a moving train crossing a massive steel bridge across a body of water. Like the heads leaning out of the train's window, we are positioned along one side of the train, looking forward. For several seconds, the speed of the train displays the power of Korea's modernity; the rivets on the thick steel bars, and a second similar bridge visible nearby, both signal major progress in the country's postwar development. The scene then cuts to the funeral, riding the momentum of the train's fast movement by zooming in to a medium shot of Sŏn-yŏng's grieving mother. It is raining hard; Sŏn-yŏng's mother crouches by the grave as others stand around holding umbrellas. As dirt is thrown on the mound, the mother decries Dong-sik for getting her daughter dismissed. Lightning strikes multiple times, saturating the screen with white light as the mother stands up and continues her tirade against Dong-sik: 'What did she ever do to you?' she wails. The sequence then cuts to Dong-sik and Kyŏng-hŭi

The train

Lightning strikes at the funeral

arriving at the Kims' house in a car at night (which, as noted earlier, is the first time we see the entire house from the outside).

This sequence repeats the editing pattern of another key moment in the film, in which the outside world (beyond the house), lightning shots that turn the screen white and reaction shots of groups of people are linked to the house through montage. Compressing the duration of an afternoon and evening into a rapid series of shots, the montage creates an accelerated rhythm that seems to reflect an accelerated modernity. Beginning in the music room – where Dong-sik had discovered Sŏn-yŏng's love letter – the events in this funeral montage are understood to be set in motion by Dong-sik's subsequent actions. In turn, the grieving and angry mother seems to give voice to the shock expressed by the factory women in the preceding scene. Importantly, the montage ends back at the house, where Dong-sik and Kyŏng-hŭi will be alone, with Dong-sik's wife and family away at his in-law's house. The montage in effect ushers in the conditions under which Kyŏng-hŭi will confess her love for Dong-sik, and then threaten to defame him when she is spurned. The funeral montage thus signals a point in the story, and the moment in modernity, in which seemingly small decisions spiral out of control. The very public mourning of the mother, coming after a shot of the train – a signature apparatus of modernity – situates Dong-sik and his entanglement in the desirous plots of a series of young factory women within these larger societal frameworks. The house to which the montage returns in the final shot of the sequence, then, is no longer the site of privacy and domesticity, but rather the contested site of Korean modernity itself.

The bar scene – beginning and ending with a montage sequence, but employing more straightforward continuity editing for the actual conversation in the middle – similarly captures the disorienting impact of modernisation, this time through the point of view of Dong-sik. The housemaid pressures him to continue their relationship more openly; his wife and children return home from visiting their grandparents; Dong-sik is losing his moral sense. Seeking advice, he goes out to meet a friend. Cutting away from a scene in which the housemaid spies on Dong-sik from the balcony, the first half of the montage sequence begins with a shot of Dong-sik walking towards the camera on a city street at night, deep in thought. It then cuts to a shot of a bartender shaking a cocktail before pouring it out for Dong-sik and his friend, Yu, both of whom appear in the mirror behind the bartender as he steps out of the frame.

Here the editing becomes more straightforward for the moment. The shot reverses to the pair, who begin to have a conversation about the legal consequences of adultery. Yu's assessment is that an affair is legally less consequential than a traffic violation, and privately

Dong-sik walks to the bar

acceptable if conducted with discretion. Dong-sik's confusion is registered in a sustained close-up of his face, distorted in puzzlement, in which we can see the bartender's hand rhythmically shaking another cocktail as Dong-sik tries to process what his friend is saying. Where the cocktail's rhythm had earlier matched the tempo of the music playing in the bar, the rattling of ice now registers Dong-sik's racing mind. His mounting anger towards Yu turns to derision as he decides he has the moral upper hand. 'You're corrupt,' he tells Yu, and leaves the bar.

The montage returns when Dong-sik hits the busy street. It is dark; he stands on the pavement as cars with lights flash by. Jazz music plays. Across the street, there is a large illuminated emblem of South Korea (a Rose of Sharon flower with five petals) low down on the door of a building with a small crowd of people standing nearby. The eye is pulled by the light of the national emblem with 'peace' written in the centre, but Dong-sik – whose bright white jacket creates the other focal point in this shot – moves away in the opposite direction, away from the symbol of authority and away from peace. He stumbles drunkenly to the kerb to hail a taxi. The scene cuts to the cab interior where we see the driver and Dong-sik, sitting in the back, framed in a single close-up shot from below. 'Where to?' the driver asks. 'Just go anywhere. Drive fast. Fly up in the air, or smash into something,' Dong-sik says, flailing at the driver. The scene cuts to a shot of the road blurry with movement and made worse by the drops of rain on the windscreen; the camera oscillates left and right as lights from the oncoming cars move in the opposite direction. It is a dizzying visual of urban disorientation. The sequence ends, again returning to the house, with a cut to a close-up of a coffee pot in the kitchen, lit by Jŏng-sim's stark white dress, which in turn is contrasted by the maid's black dress. We learn now that the housemaid is pregnant as the smell of coffee makes her feel sick.

The juxtaposition – a discussion about morality and disorienting modernity – is clear enough. Dong-sik's failings as a husband are here aligned to the historical transformation that

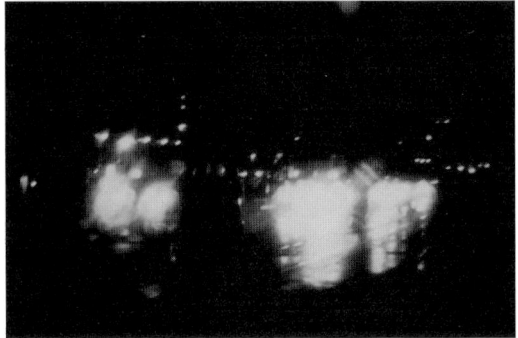

Dong-sik hails a cab; dizzying blurry road; the housemaid realises she is pregnant

is becoming visible on the city streets. His increasingly disturbed psychological state is turned into visual spectacle, registered in relation to the speeding cars in the frenzied rhythms of jazz music and cocktail shakers. If the funeral montage compresses narrative time in a sequence of quick, stylised shots and zoom effects, Dong-sik's drunkenness in the bar scene montage expresses discomfort with acceleration, as manifested by the new pace of urban life. In both cases, Dong-sik cannot seem to keep up with the accelerations.

After the housemaid moves into the house, we have Jŏng-sim's dream scene, a quick montage of sorts, in which she sees dying rats with human heads. This would seem to indicate her subconscious manifestation of the porosity of the house walls, and the inextricability of the domestic space from the broader world in which it exists. The housemaid has an acute sense of smell, and she is drawn by the smell of curry to the kitchen, where she finds a rat in a cupboard, kills it with a club and is told to use the rat poison instead. She prepares a plate of rice with rat poison, which she inhales deeply before placing it on the floor, and is shown up to her room. Then Dong-sik goes across the hall for his piano lesson with Kyŏng-hŭi. Hearing the piano music, the maid walks across the veranda and peers in through the window, watching Dong-sik's interactions with

The housemaid finds a rat in the kitchen after she arrives at the house

Jŏng-sim's dream of rats on a plate

Kyŏng-hŭi during their lesson. The scene then cuts to Jŏng-sim's dream. In the actual shot of the rats squirming on the plate of curry rice they do not have human heads, and we know this detail only from her account of the dream to Dong-sik; it is unclear who the two rats in her dream represent. According to Kim Ho-yŏng, the maid's infiltration of the house likens her to the rats, as they occupy the same space of the kitchen.[107] Rendering the maid as a 'rat woman' by such associations, Pak U-sŏng argues, is meant to trigger fear in spectators.[108] Sorting out the referents is difficult because the montage infers but does not show Jŏng-sim's actual dream. We can conjecture, however, that the violent dream foreshadows the violent end of the film, in which several characters die, some of whom by ingesting rat poison.

Given the violent future this dream portends, it is notable that the conversation between Dong-sik and Jŏng-sim after she describes her dream quickly turns to a far more optimistic vision of the future. She speaks about not wanting to rent out any of the rooms in their new house and how she would like another son and to send their children to college. This ambivalent pairing of middle-class ambition with violent death (as manifested in the spectacle of the poisoned rats) should not go unnoticed. Indeed, ambition and violent tragedy are strongly linked in *Hanyŏ*. In the world imagined by the film, our desires – whether material, for a new house, or piano or television, or for more

inchoate objects like love, comfort and security – cannot be pursued
without conflict, violence and death. For this reason, in addition to
her nightmare, Jŏng-sim's other characteristic physical reaction to
the challenges of modern domestic life – her dizziness – elaborates
Hanyŏ's broader depiction of emergent Korean modernity. Just as
Jŏng-sim gets dizzy when scared by the sight of a rat in her cupboards,
she is also made dizzy through her determined labour. In turn, this
physical disorientation is doubled by the various montage scenes
discussed in this chapter; throughout, the accelerations of modernity
affect temporal compressions that leave characters and audiences
spinning. Montage in its various forms allowed Kim Ki-young to create
frisson by bringing together fragmented, heterogeneous elements in
compacted sequences, which mimicked the harried feeling caused
by the compressed modernisation emerging in the 1960s. Montage
in *Hanyŏ* became a mode for representing the social transformation
characteristic of its historical moment in sensory and emotive terms,
and in the process attempted to reorganise existing ways of seeing.

The widely circulated 'Kill that bitch!' anecdote with which
this chapter began manifests the ambivalence of frisson. The sense
of shock was shared by critics outside South Korea in its later
reception as well. *Hanyŏ*'s discovery, wrote Jean-Michel Frodon,
the editor-in-chief of *Cahiers du cinéma*, in his 2003 entry in the
book *1001 Movies You Must See Before You Die*, 'is a marvelous
feeling – marvelous not just because one finds in writer-director Kim
Ki-young a truly extraordinary image-maker, but in his film such an
utterly unpredictable work'. Frodon attributed the shocking nature
of the film to the 'intensity of the passion' between the characters,
achieved through various stylistic choices, such as 'the unusual length
of one of the director's shots, by his pop-art use of everyday objects,
or by the invading presence of the human (feminine) body', which
succeeded in opening 'the door to new sensations for the viewer'.[109]
In reorganising ways of seeing, the compressed aesthetics of *Hanyŏ*
not only registered the pressures of rapid industrialisation in sensory
terms, they also gestured to new ways of feeling.

Coda: *Hanyŏ*'s Afterlife

As Dong-sik's final address to the viewer suggests, *Hanyŏ* would like us to believe that the story it is telling is a moral one. A story that instructs us to resist the temptations of modernisation, that reveals how modernity's attractions are invariably accompanied by dark consequences. But in offering – at the very last minute – this simplistic moral vision, the film makes us aware of what is ultimately its more important insight: that modernisation entails alternative ways of seeing. Made at a postwar moment when modernisation seemed possible – sitting on the horizon but not yet realised – *Hanyŏ* reminds us that modernity has to be imagined before it can be lived. In such an uncertain epistemological milieu, the film thus compels its audience to reconceptualise how reality is constituted, and, in the midst of Korea's compressed modernity, what shape it might take in the years to come.

The figure of the housemaid – not just her fate, but even her very body – becomes in the film a site in which viewers explore emergent logics of industrialisation and urbanisation. The resulting exploration gets messy and confuses socio-economic transformations with sexual transgression. Thus, as this book has argued, *Hanyŏ* was a precursor, imagining a nascent aesthetics of a compressed modernity – part projection, part fantasy – that did not yet exist, but would soon gather momentum in the mid-1960s under the dictatorial rule of Park Chung-hee. The repercussions of this momentum still reverberate into the present day. In both anticipating a new reality and taking part in its construction, the film offers a vision that is uncanny in its prescience: we see the clumsy emergence of a newly burgeoning middle class, with its dramatic recalibrations of class, gender and power. This uncanny vision, in turn, helps us understand the remarkable afterlife of a film that, initially, seemed unlikely to have an afterlife at all.

Beginning with its release at an uncertain historical moment and its re-emergence in another, *Hanyŏ* has lived a few distinct lives as a film. In each of these historical iterations, the film has challenged us to question the era's social mores and standards for existing norms of visual representation. In 1960, the film's first life was characterised by its brazen depiction of a distinctively unstable social order, which bound nascent modern desires to moral depravity in shocking fashion. But more than merely occasioning moral caution, *Hanyŏ* constructed a world out of these unsettling components. Invoking modern architecture to develop a new spatial sense, *Hanyŏ* deployed its forms, scales and methods in conjunction with techniques of film that condensed the image and compressed the narrative to construct an image space for the psyche within film that would become characteristic of South Korean films concerned with social class. The film implied a remapping of class relations while providing a new filmic vocabulary in Korean cinema with which to discuss that remapping. But despite this initial flame, the film soon faded from memory, was largely forgotten for the next thirty years and was nearly lost to history.

Although Kim Ki-young continued to be recognised as a master film-maker within the Korean film industry, he otherwise gradually slipped into obscurity. That descent began with his struggles under stringent censorship, as the series of Korea's dictatorships clamped down on his creative endeavours and forced him to make compromises that ultimately made it difficult to replicate the commercial success of his early housemaid films. Television had also become popular and the many restrictions on importing Hollywood films were lifted, further diminishing the centrality of Korean cinema. Then in the mid- to late 1990s, Korean film culture experienced a revival, on the heels of a cinematic new wave and the subsequent success of more popular Korean cinema thereafter. As the internet emerged, so too did impassioned film communities online. Film buffs connected to explore lesser-known cult films. Film festivals were established not only to celebrate the new breadth of Korean film production in the period, but also as critical spaces to explore social issues and identity, under the rubric of what film critic Soyoung Kim has described as 'cine-mania', a Korean version of cinephilia that displaced the site of political fervour (previously located in democratisation activism) onto the festivals – 'a shift in the site of Korean activism from the politico-economic to the cultural sphere'.[110]

The rediscovery of *Hanyŏ* in 1997 was thus timely, insofar as it provided an important precursor, and even a point of origin, for the flowering of Korean cinema at the turn of the twenty-first century. *Hanyŏ* had previously not been released on VHS due to two missing reels, and it was largely through the VHS circulation of Kim's own remakes of *Hanyŏ* – first *Hwanyŏ* in 1971, and then *Hwanyŏ '82* in 1982 – that young film-makers such as Bong Joon Ho and Park Chan-wook, who would go on to represent a South Korean film renaissance, had become familiar with his housemaid films. But it was only the discovery of a new release print of the full original that enabled it to eventually be screened as part of a Kim Ki-young retrospective at the newly founded Busan International Film Festival in 1997. Sadly, Kim Ki-young died suddenly in a house fire on 6 February 1998, just as he was anticipating a major global career revival. The fervent mythologisation of Kim Ki-young began almost immediately after his death.

It is not surprising, then, that an entire generation of Korean film-makers have cited *Hanyŏ* as one of the most influential films for their careers, and in some cases, specifically on their films that deal with issues of class and gender. The most obvious example is Im Sang-soo's adaptation of *Hanyŏ* (2010), and his loosely based sequel, *Ton ŭi mat*. Equally shaped by *Hanyŏ* have been Park Chan-wook's period piece *Agassi* (*The Handmaiden*, 2016), set in Japanese-occupied Korea, and Bong Joon Ho's film about wealth disparity, *Parasite*, which won four Academy Awards in 2020. In the penultimate scene of Im's *Hanyŏ*, the house goes up in flames as the fraught housemaid shuns the symbolic staircase, and its descent

Kim Ki-young at the 1997 BIFF hand-printing ceremony
(courtesy Busan International Film Festival)

towards death, and instead hangs herself on a chandelier and catches
fire. The final scene finds the family outdoors, where a couch, chairs
and artwork are arranged as if in a living room indoors, celebrating
their daughter Nami's birthday. As a result of the housemaid's
actions, the house and housemaid, the objects of wealth that filled the
house and the melodramatic narrative of class mobility have engulfed
and subsumed each other in the fire. The walls dissolve altogether.
The transparent windows, so central to Kim Ki-young's 1960
Hanyŏ, have been entirely eliminated. These final moments replicate

the theatricality and performativity of the ending of Kim's *Hanyŏ*, similarly drawing attention to the distinct presence of film as medium and its capacity to modify not just representations of the middle class but also how we see such representations. On the one hand, the domestic setting recreated outside the house renders the iconic site of the middle-class home portrayed in the original *Hanyŏ* as no longer adequate to contain persistent class tensions. On the other hand, that domestic setting remains so resonant because of *Hanyŏ*'s iconic narrative.

A few years later, Im took even more creative liberties, but without losing hold of *Hanyŏ*'s legacy. Im's *Ton ŭi mat*, about neoliberal wealth, radically restructures the *Hanyŏ* narrative on two levels: through gender reversal (Korea's corporate employees *are* the housemaid, as one character states), and through a reversal of the private and public spheres, such that the domestic space now contains the socio-economic world that, a half-century earlier, had lain outside the middle-class home. The emergent ways of seeing into the psyche of a compressed society that the original *Hanyŏ* forced upon us are here turned onto contemporary society, by literally and metaphorically domesticating it in order to encourage still-new ways of seeing, much as *Hanyŏ* did in 1960, but now in a Korea far removed from its compressed modernity but where those same ills still persist. Bong's *Parasite*, from 2020, is a useful final example of the meaning-generating ways in which the material-semiotic reconstitutes the boundaries of bodies and objects and affirms newly materialising boundaries. *Parasite* deploys *Hanyŏ*'s experimentation with genres – in particular crime, horror and melodrama – to defy existent formulations of genre, and also emulates its exploration of cinematic architecture as a means to render class conflict. Here again we have a multi-storey house, contained by floor-to-ceiling windows and bound by stairs. Bong has called *Parasite* a 'staircase movie',[111] where 'the stairs are as important as the characters'[112] in what they symbolise. The homage is clear. Just like Kim Ki-young's corporealisation of the set and of the inanimate world, here the architectural features function like – and interact with – the bodies that traverse, ascend and descend them, as both architectural features and bodies reconstitute boundaries.

Kim Ki-young's impact extends far beyond directors; his presence in the South Korean film industry as a whole has been manifold. In 2021, the veteran Korean actress Youn Yuh-jung became the first Korean actor to win an Academy Award. For her role in the film *Minari* (dir. Lee Isaac Chung, 2020), she won both the Oscar as well as a BAFTA for Best Supporting Actress. In her speech, she thanked director Kim Ki-young, who first cast her in her breakout roles in the *Hanyŏ* sequels *Hwanyŏ* and *The Insect Woman*. The acknowledgment of Kim Ki-young by directors and actresses in their global accomplishments today is testament to the director's legacy and continued relevance.

Kim Ki-young (courtesy Korean Film Archive)

Notes

1 A note on romanisation: Korean
names and titles are romanised
following the McCune-Reischauer
system, except in cases where proper
nouns including names already have
an established presence or preferred
spelling known to English-speaking
audiences, either through self-
representation or common usage.
2 Yi Yŏn-ho, *Hanyŏ* DVD booklet,
Re-birth of the Classics: Hanyŏ (Korean
Film Archive Collection, 2009), p. 29.
3 See Chang Kyung-sup, 'Compressed
Modernity and its Discontents: South
Korean Society in Transition', *Economy
and Society* 28 no. 1 (1999), pp. 30–55.
4 Chang Kyung-sup, 'Compressed
Modernity in South Korea: Constitutive
Dimensions, Manifesting Units, and
Historical Conditions', in Youna Kim
(ed.), *Routledge Handbook of Korean Culture
and Society* (New York: Routledge, 2016),
pp. 31–47, p. 33.
5 Chun Soonok, *They Are Not Machines:
Korean Women Workers and Their Fight for
Democratic Trade Unionism in the 1970s*
(London: Routledge, 2003), p. 14.
6 Bruce Cumings, *Korea's Place in the Sun:
A Modern History* (New York: W. W.
Norton, 1998), p. 351.
7 Chun, *They Are Not Machines*, pp. 12–13.
8 Ibid., pp. 14–15.
9 John Kie-chiang Oh, *Korean Politics: The
Quest for Democratization and Economic
Development* (Ithaca, NY: Cornell
University Press, 2018), pp. 43–4.
10 Arita Shin, 'The Growth of the
Korean Middle Class and its Social
Consciousness', *The Developing
Economies* XLI no. 2 (June 2003),
pp. 201–20, p. 204.
11 Ibid.

12 Travis Workman, *Political Moods:
Film Melodrama and the Cold War in the
Two Koreas* (Oakland: University of
California Press, 2023), p. 149.
13 Heather Heffner, '"A Dragon Risen
from a Shallow Stream": The South
Korean Middle Class Framed Through
Narratives of Loss, Progress, and
Return', *Alternatives: Global, Local,
Political* 40 no. 1 (February 2015),
pp. 31–45, p. 31.
14 Yi Dae-bŏm and Chŏng Su-wan,
'"Outsiders", the Symbol of Compressed
Modernization in the Housemaid
Trilogies' ['*Hanyŏyŏnjage nat'anan
apch'ukchŏg kŭndaehwaŭi tamjich'erosŏ
oebuin*'], *CineForum* [*Ssinep'orŏm*] no. 28
(2017), pp. 37–73, p. 43.
15 Ibid.
16 Ibid.
17 Hagen Koo, 'Rethinking
Korea's Middle Class' ['*Han'gugŭi
chungsanch'ŭngŭl tashi saenggak'anda*'],
*The Quarterly Changbi (Creation and
Criticism)* [*Ch'angjakkwabip'yŏng*] 40 no. 1
(2012), pp. 403–21, pp. 405–6.
18 Yi and Chŏng, '"Outsiders"', p. 46.
19 Nikki J. Y. Lee and Julian Stringer,
'Remake, Repeat, Revive: Kim Ki-young's
Housemaid Trilogies', in Claire Perkins
and Constantine Verevis (eds), *Film
Trilogies: New Critical Approaches*
(Basingstoke and New York: Palgrave
Macmillan, 2012), pp. 145–63, pp. 150–3.
20 Ibid., p. 149.
21 Yi Hyo-in, 'Biography', in Kim Hong-
joon (ed.), *Kim Ki-young* (Seoul: Korean
Film Council, 2006), p. 104.
22 Chris Berry, 'Scream and Scream
Again', in Frances Gateward (ed.),
*Seoul Searching: Culture and Identity in
Contemporary Korean Cinema* (Albany:

State University of New York Press, 2007), pp. 99–114, pp. 102–3.

23 Ibid.

24 Ibid., p. 101.

25 Alison Peirse and Daniel Martin, *Korean Horror Cinema* (Edinburgh: Edinburgh University Press, 2013), p. 4.

26 Donna Haraway, 'Situated Knowledges: The Science Question in Feminism and the Privilege of Partial Perspective', *Feminist Studies* 14 no. 3 (Autumn 1988), pp. 575–99, p. 595.

27 Stacy Alaimo and Susan Hekman (eds), *Material Feminisms* (Bloomington: Indiana University Press, 2008), p. 4.

28 See Lee and Stringer, 'Remake, Repeat, Revive', p. 150.

29 Steve Choe, 'Kim Ki-young's Housemaid Films', in Chung-kang Kim (ed.), *The Films of Kim Ki-young* (Edinburgh: Edinburgh University Press, 2023), pp. 92–3.

30 Kim Ki-young cited in Kim Hong-joon (ed.), *Kim Ki-young* (Seoul: Korean Film Council, 2006), p. 83.

31 Choe, 'Kim Ki-young's Housemaid Films', pp. 102–3.

32 For a detailed discussion of *Hanyŏ*'s restoration, see Kyung Hyun Kim, 'The Housemaid: Crossing Borders', *Criterion Essays*, 16 December 2013. Available at: <https://www.criterion.com/current/posts/2993-the-housemaid-crossing-borders> (accessed 18 November 2024).

33 Kim Ki-young, 'Chu Jŭng-nyŏ's Performance and Life' ['*Kamdogi pon chujungnyŏ: chujungnyŏŭi yŏn'giwa sasaenghwal: chŏnahan pumwigiŭi yŏn'gi-yŏnghwa hanyŏrŭl chungsimŭro*'], *Kukje Yŏnghwa* [International Film] (August 1960), pp. 122–3, p. 122.

34 Ibid.

35 Ibid., pp. 122–3.

36 Kim Ki-young, 'A Film Director's Star Theory' ['*Yŏnghwa kamdogŭi sŭt'aron*'], *The Monthly Cinema* [*Wolgan Yŏnghwa*] (December 1984), pp. 36–7, p. 36.

37 Ibid., p. 37.

38 'Attempted Notable Experiment Director Kim Ki-young's *Hanyŏ*' ['*Misuhaessuna jumokhal silhŏm kim ki-yŏng gamdok ŭi hanyŏ*'], *Tonga Ilbo*, 9 November 1960.

39 Ibid.

40 Kim (ed.), *Kim Ki-young*, p. 70.

41 Yi Yŏn-ho, 'Director Kim Ki-young: Half a Century of Solitude and Love of Thirty-one Films' ['*Kim Kiyŏng gamdok banbaeknyŏnŭi godokkwa sŏrŭn hanaŭi yŏnghwa sarang*'], *KINO* (January 1997). For the English translation see Kim (ed.), *Kim Ki-young*, p. 73.

42 Kwŏn Podŭrae and Ch'ŏn Chŏnghwan, *To Question the 1960s* [*1960-yŏn ŭl mutta: Pak Chŏng-hŭi sidae ŭi munhwa chŏngch'i wa chisŏng*] (Seoul: Ch'ŏnnyŏnŭi Sangsang [Imagine 1000], 2012), pp. 402–3.

43 Kim (ed.), *Kim Ki-young*, pp. 72–3.

44 Mok Hae-jung, 'A Comparative Analysis of Sound in Kim Ki-young's *The Housemaid* and Im Sang-soo's *The Housemaid*' ['*Kim Kiyŏng Hanyŏwa Im Sangsu Hanyŏŭi saundŭ pigyo punsŏk*'], *CineForum* [*Ssinep'orŏm*] 11 (2010), pp. 61–96, p. 71.

45 Michel Chion, *Audio-Vision: Sound on Screen* (New York: Columbia University Press, 2019), p. 5.

46 See Yu Ji-hyŏng (ed.), *24 Years of Conversation: Interviews with Director Kim Ki-young* [*Isipsanyŏngan ŭi daehwa: Kim Ki-young gamdok intŏbyujip*] (Seoul: Sun, 2006), pp. 81–2.

47 Kim (ed.), *Kim Ki-young*, p. 70.
48 Kim Ki-young interview in Yu (ed.), *24 Years of Conversation*, pp. 87–8.
49 Ibid., p. 82.
50 Ibid., pp. 87–8.
51 Ibid., p. 88.
52 Ibid., p. 82.
53 Ibid.
54 See Kim Sŏn-jin, 'A Study on the Recognition of Modernity in the Film *The Housemaid*' ['*Yŏnghwa hanyŏŭi kŭndaesŏng inshig yŏn'gu*'], *Journal of Digital Design* [*Tijit'ŏltijainhak yŏn'gu*] 11 no. 1 (2011), pp. 91–100, pp. 93–9. Mun So-jŏng, 'Reflections on the Modernity of the Korean Family' ['*Han'guk kajogŭi kŭndaesŏnge taehan sŏngch'al*'], in The Institute for Korean Historical Studies [*Yŏksamunjeyŏn'guso*] (ed.), *Clash Between Tradition and the West* [*Chŏnt'onggwa sŏguŭi ch'ungdol*] (Goyang: Yŏksabip'yŏngsa, 2001); and Kim Sŏng-gi, *What is Modernity?* [*Modŏnit'iran muŏshin'ga*] (Seoul: Minŭmsa, 1994).
55 The censorship materials were donated by the Korean Media Research Institute (KMRI), which had organised the materials they received from the Korea Media Rating Board [*Yŏngsangmul Tŭnggŭp Wiwonhoe*].
56 Hye Seung Chung, 'Fending Off Darkness, Uplifting National Cinema: Korean Film Censorship and The Stray Bullet', *Situations* 16 no. 1 (31 March 2023), pp. 1–28, p. 10.
57 Korean Film Archive, Kim Ki-young Censorship Materials Collection [*Kim Kiyŏng Kŏmyŏljaryo K'ŏlleksyŏn*]. Available at: <https://www.kmdb.or.kr/collectionlist/itemDetailPop?dataId=171&typeClss=CE&colName=&colId=281&isLooked=false> (accessed 18 November 2024).
58 Chung, 'Fending Off Darkness', p. 27n19.
59 Ibid.
60 Min Eungjun, Joo Jinsook and Kwak Han Ju, *Korean Film: History, Resistance, and Democratic Imagination* (Westport, CT: Praeger, 2003), p. 47.
61 Cho Junhyoung, 'An Early Liberation Zone? The Emergence and Dissolution of the National Motion Picture Ethics Committee' ['*Ttae Irŭn Haebang-gu? Yŏnghwayullijŏn'gugwiwŏnhoeŭi Tŭngjanggwa Haech'e*'], *Webzine*, Research Institute of Korean Studies, 19 August 2014. Available at: <http://rikszine.korea.ac.kr/front/article/humanList.minyeon?selectArticle_id=505&selectCategory_id=61> (accessed 23 November 2022).
62 'Restoration of Foreign Film Censorship System, Strict Due Diligence Screening, Crackdown on Obscene Films' ['*Oehwa kŏmyŏlchedo puhwal, shilsashimsarŭl ŏmgyŏk'i, ch'ujap'an yŏnghwanŭn tansokk'iro*'], *Seoul Sinmun*, 18 October 1960.
63 'Ethics Seen in Recent Movies, Dialogue Between Audience and Writer' ['*Yojŭm yŏnghwaesŏ pon yulli, kwan'gaekkwa chakkaŭi taehwa*'], *Tonga Ilbo*, 4 November 1960.
64 According to Cho Junhyoung, in January 1961, NMPEC and the MoE clashed again as controversy arose over the public screening of Edmond T. Gréville's 1960 British teen exploitation film, *Beat Girl* (Korean title *Young Bodies*; released in the US as *Wild for Kicks*). *Beat Girl* contained topless nudity, juvenile delinquency and teenagers playing

'chicken' with oncoming trains. On 21 January 1961, the screening of *Beat Girl* became the first case since the April Revolution of 1960 that the NMPEC voted to defer. Despite the ongoing investigation, the MoE permitted the screening of *Beat Girl* on 15 February, with 320 feet deleted. The tensions between the MoE and the FEC escalated until an agreement, laying out their respective roles and reorganising the process of foreign film import, was reached in March 1961. See Cho, 'Early Liberation Zone?' and 'Policy to Ban Screening of *Young Bodies* Due to Concerns About Trouble with Young Bodies and Negative Social Impact', *Hankuk Ilbo*, 28 January 1961.

65 Cho, 'Early Liberation Zone?' cites 'Restoration of Foreign Film Censorship System, Strict Due Diligence Screening, Crackdown on Obscene Films', *Seoul Sinmun*, 18 October 1960.

66 Cho, 'Early Liberation Zone?' cites 'NMPEC on Verge of Existence' ['*Chonp'yeŭi kiroe sŏn yŏngnyun*'], *Chosŏn Ilbo*, 22 February 1961. See also, 'Strict Crackdown on Adultery Movie, Correction of the Import Recommendation Procedure of the Ministry of Education' ['*Pullyunŭi yŏnghwa kangnyŏk'i tansok, munkyobu suipch'uch'ŏnjŏlch'arŭl shijŏng*'], *Kyunghyang Sinmun*, 26 October 1960, p. 3.

67 'Strict Crackdown on Adultery Movies', p. 3.

68 Chung, 'Fending Off Darkness', p. 2.

69 Ibid.

70 Lee Soon-jin, 'Obaltan (Yu Hyŏn-mok, 1961), Censored Documents Lifted' ['*Obalt'an (Yu Hyŏnmok, 1961) kŏmyŏl sŏryu haeje*'], KMDb, 28 January 2018.

Available at: <https://www.kmdb.or.kr/history/contents/1706> (accessed 18 November 2024).

71 Ibid.

72 See Shin Jŏng-ch'ŏl, '[Conversations with Directors] Kim Ki-young, Veteran Director Pursuing a New World in Works' ['*Yŏnghwagamdokkwaŭi taedam] Kim Kiyŏng, saeroun chakp'umsegyerŭl ch'uguhanŭn nojang kamdok*'], *The Monthly Cinema* [*Wŏlgan Yŏnghwa*] (October 1984), p. 55.

73 'Kim Ki-young for Best Director' ['*Kamdoksange Kim Kiyŏngssi*'], *Chosŏn Ilbo*, 3 May 1961, p. 4.

74 'Domestic Quality Film Awards' ['*Kuksan usu yŏnghwasang*'], *Chosŏn Ilbo*, 29 December 1961, p. 3.

75 <https://www.kmdb.or.kr/db/kor/detail/movie/K/00609> (accessed 18 November 2024).

76 Vivian Sobchack, 'Afterword: Media Archaeology and Re-presencing the Past', in Erkki Huhtamo and Jussi Parikka (eds), *Media Archaeology: Approaches, Applications, and Implications* (Los Angeles: University of California Press, 2011), pp. 323–33, p. 323.

77 See Yi Hyo-in, *Thirteen Korean Film Directors* [*Hangukŭi yŏnghwa gamdok 13-in*] (Paju: Yŏllinch'aektŭl, 1994), p. 363; and selections from interviews in Kim (ed.), *Kim Ki-young*, p. 67.

78 Kim (ed.), *Kim Ki-young*, p. 67.

79 Yi Ch'ŏl-chae, 'A Study on Characteristics of Interior Space in Korean Classic Films – Space in 1960s Homes as Seen in the Expressionist film *Hanyŏ*' ['*Han'guk kojŏnyŏnghwarŭl t'onghae pon shillae konggan t'ŭksŏnge kwanhan yŏn'gu – p'yohyŏnjuŭi yŏnghwa hanyŏe nat'anan 1960nyŏndae*

chut'aekkongganŭl chungshimŭro'],
Korean Institute of Interior Design Journal
[*Hanguksillaedijainhak'oe nonmunjip*]
21 no. 2 (April 2012), pp. 65–73.
80 Han Sang Kim, '"My" Sweet Home
in the Next Decade: The Popular
Imagination of Private Homeownership
during the Yusin Period', in Youngju
Ryu (ed.), *Cultures of Yusin: South Korea
in the 1970s* (Ann Arbor: University of
Michigan Press, 2018), pp. 119–40, p. 119.
81 Kim Ye-Rim, 'The Cultural Politics
of Developmental Nationalism and
Middle-Class Home Fantasy in the
Late 1960s' ['*1960-yŏndae chunghuban
kaebal naesyŏnŏllijum kwa chungsanch'ŭng
kajŏng p'ant'aji ŭi munhwa chŏngch'ihak*'],
Journal of Korean Modern Literature
[*Hyŏndae munhakŭi yŏn'gu*] 32 (2007),
pp. 339–75.
82 Mun Kŭn-chong, 'A Study on Images
of Apartment Housing in Korean Films
in the 1930s–60s' ['*1930–60 nyŏndae
han'guk yŏnghwae nat'ananŭn ap'at'ŭ
imiji yŏn'gu*'], *Journal of the Architectural
Institute of Korea* [*Taehan'gŏnch'uk'ak'oe
nonmunjip*] (January 2013), pp. 147–58.
83 Kim (ed.), *Kim Ki-young*, p. 72.
84 Ibid.
85 Anne Friedberg, *The Virtual Window:
From Alberti to Microsoft* (Cambridge, MA:
MIT Press, 2009), p. 1.
86 Le Corbusier, cited by Beatriz Colomina
in *Privacy and Publicity: Modern Architecture
as Mass Media* (Cambridge, MA: MIT Press,
1994), p. 7 [italics in original].
87 Ibid.
88 Ibid., p. 6.
89 Anthony Vidler, 'The Explosion of
Space: Architecture and the Filmic
Imaginary', *Assemblage* no. 21 (August
1993), pp. 45–59, p. 46.

90 See Hong Jin-hyuk, 'The Housemaid's
Expressionist Mise-en-scène and
Modernism – A Style Analysis of
Vertical Lines' ['*Hanyŏŭi p'yohyŏnjuŭi
mijangsen'gwa modŏnijŭm – sujiksŏnŭl
chungshimŭro han sŭt'ail punsŏk*'], *The
Korean Journal of Arts Studies* [*Hanguk
yesul yŏn'gu*] no. 16 (2017), pp. 239–64.
91 Kim Ki-young considered lighting
to be one of the most important tools
at his disposal when making a film.
His earlier film *Box of Death* (1955),
although the first Korean film to feature
simultaneous recording [*dongsi nokum
ch'waryong*], had been a disappointment
for Kim in terms of the lighting, falling
short of the films he had seen in Japan
as a student. The problem with his
lighting had been pointed out to him
by a Japanese lighting technician, and
he was able to get help from someone
who had studied lighting in Japan and,
on future films, from another contact
who had a photo shop in Jinhae. See Yi,
Thirteen Korean Film Directors, p. 363.
92 Yu (ed.), *24 Years of Conversation*, p. 87.
93 Chris Berry, 'The Housemaid (1960):
Possessed by the Dispossessed', in
Sangjoon Lee (ed.), *Rediscovering Korean
Cinema* (Ann Arbor: University of
Michigan Press, 2019), pp. 147–59, p. 153.
See also Peirse and Martin (eds), *Korean
Horror Cinema*, p. 4.
94 Yi, *Thirteen Korean Film Directors*, p. 364.
95 David Bordwell, 'You Are My Density',
blog post, davidbordwell.net,
1 November 2011. Available at:
<https://www.davidbordwell.net/
blog/2011/11/01/you-are-my-density/>
(accessed 18 November 2024).
96 Ibid.
97 Chang, 'Compressed Modernity', p. 33.

98 Soyoung Kim, 'Questions of Woman's Film', in Kathleen McHugh and Nancy Abelmann (eds), *South Korean Golden Age Melodrama* (Detroit, MI: Wayne State University Press, 2005), pp. 185–200, p. 191. Citing an interview with Kim Ki-young by Soyoung Kim for the *PIFF Daily News*, 2nd Busan International Film Festival, 13 October 1997.

99 Ana Hedberg Olenina, *Psychomotor Aesthetics: Movement and Affect in Modern Literature and Film* (Oxford: Oxford University Press, 2020), p. 174. Olenina translates and cites from Sergei Eisenstein's 1929 'Kak delaetsia pafos?', RGALI (the Russian State Archive of Literature and Arts), f. 1923 op.1 ed. khr. 793 l. 31.

100 Sergei Eisenstein, 'Word and Image', in Eisenstein, *Film Sense*, ed. and trans. Jay Leyda (New York: Harcourt Brace & Company, 1947), p. 17.

101 Christian Suhr and Rane Willerslev, 'Introduction: Montage as an Amplifier of Invisibility', in Suhr and Willerslev (eds), *Transcultural Montage* (New York: Berghahn Books, 2013), pp. 1–16, p. 1.

102 Pak Yŏngmin, 'Film Study: *Hanyŏ*' ['*Chakp'umyŏn'gu: 'Hanyŏ'*'], *Kukje Yŏnghwa* [International Film] (1961; March issue, published 1 February), p. 67.

103 Ibid.

104 Ibid.

105 Cynthia Baron, 'Acting Choices/Filmic Choices: Rethinking Montage and Performance', *Journal of Film and Video* 59 no. 2 (Summer 2007), p. 33.

106 David Bordwell, 'The Idea of Montage in Soviet Art and Film', *Cinema Journal* 11 no. 2 (1972), pp. 9–17, p. 9.

107 Kim Ho-yŏng, 'Pre-modernity in Modernity: A Study of Space in Kim Ki-young's Films' ['*Kim Kiyŏng yŏnghwaŭi konggan kujoe nat'ananŭn kŭndaewa chŏn'gŭndaeŭi kaltŭngyangsang*'], *Semiotic Inquiry* [*Gihohak yŏn'gu*] 20 (December 2006), pp. 199–229, p. 205.

108 Pak U-sŏng, 'The Performativity and Position of Rats in *The Housemaid*' ['*Hanyŏ esŏ chwiranŭn changch'iga suhaenghanŭn yŏk'algwa wisang – Kim Kiyŏng shinhwaŭi pip'anjŏg chaegorŭl wihan ilgoch'al*'], *Film Studies* [*Yŏnghwa yŏn'gu*] 49 (September 2011), pp. 69–76.

109 Jean-Michel Frodon, '*Hanyŏ the Housemaid*, Kim Ki-young, 1960', in Steven Jay Schneider (ed.), *1001 Movies You Must See Before You Die* (Denver, CO: Peterson's Publishing), p. 373.

110 Soyoung Kim, '"Cine-mania" or Cinephilia: Film Festivals and the Identity Question', in Chi-Yun Shin and Julian Stringer (eds), *New Korean Cinema* (Edinburgh: Edinburgh University Press, 2005), p. 79. Reprinted from *UTS Review* (now *Cultural Studies Review*) 4 no. 2 (1998), pp. 174–87.

111 E. Alex Jung, 'The House That *Parasite* Built (From Scratch)', *Vulture*, 4 February 2020. Available at: <https://www.vulture.com/2020/02/how-bong-joon-ho-built-the-houses-in-parasite.html> (accessed 18 November 2024).

112 The Criterion Channel, 'Bong Joon Ho on *The Housemaid*', 17 December 2013. Available at: <https://www.criterion.com/current/posts/3002-bong-joon-ho-on-the-housemaid> (accessed 18 November 2024).

Credits

Hanyŏ/The Housemaid
Republic of Korea
1960

Directed by
Kim Ki-young
Production Company
Korean Literature Film
Co., Ltd
Kim Ki-young
Productions
Produced by
Kim Ki-young
Production Executive
Kim Yŏng-chŏl
Screenplay
Kim Ki-young
Cinematography
Kim Dŏk-jin
Lighting
Ko Hae-jin
Editor
Oh Yŏng-gŭn
Music
Han Sang-ki
Art Director
Pak Sŏg-in
**Sound Editor
(Recording)**
Son In-ho
Sound Editor (Effects)
Yi Sang-man
Assistant Directors
Chŏn Ŭng-ju
Kim Dae-hŭi
Chŏng Hyo-sŏp

Scripter
Kim Jŏng-suk
Production Manager
An Sŏk-jin
Cinematography Team
Yu Yŏng-jo
Yi Sŭng-ŏn
Ch'oe Sŭng-hak
Lighting Team
Sŏ Byŏng-su
Kim Dong-p'o

CAST
Kim Jin-kyu
Dong-sik
Chu Jŭng-nyŏ
Jŏng-sim, Dong-sik's wife
Yi Ŭn-sim
the housemaid
Ŏm Aeng-ran
Cho Kyŏng-hŭi
Ok Kyŏng-hŭi
Kwak Sŏn-yŏng
An Sŏng-gi
Ch'ang-sun, the son
Yi Yu-ri
Ae-sun, the daughter
Kang Sŏk-che
Wang Sung-nang
Ko Sŏn-ae
Na Jŏng-ok
Na Ok-chu
Ch'oe Nam-hyŏn
Cho Sŏk-kŭn
Nam Bang-ch'un
Kim Man

Production Details
35mm
1.37:1
Black and white
Mono
Running time:
108 minutes

Release Details
Republic of Korea
theatrical release on
3 November 1960

Bibliography

Alaimo, Stacy and Susan Hekman (eds), *Material Feminisms* (Bloomington: Indiana University Press, 2008).

'Attempted Notable Experiment Director Kim Ki-young's *Hanyŏ*' ['*Misuhaessuna jumokhal silhŏm kim ki-young gamdok ui hanyŏ*'], *Tonga Ilbo*, 9 November 1960.

Baron, Cynthia, 'Acting Choices/Filmic Choices: Rethinking Montage and Performance', *Journal of Film and Video* 59 no. 2 (Summer 2007), pp. 32–40.

Berry, Chris, 'Introducing "Mr. Monster": Kim Ki-young and the Critical Economy of the Globalized Art-House Cinema', in Kim Hong-joon (ed.), *Kim Ki-young* (Seoul: Korean Film Council, 2006), pp. 41–53.

Berry, Chris, 'Scream and Scream Again', in Frances Gateward (ed.), *Seoul Searching: Culture and Identity in Contemporary Korean Cinema* (Albany: State University of New York Press, 2007), pp. 99–114.

Berry, Chris, 'The Housemaid (1960): Possessed by the Dispossessed', in Sangjoon Lee (ed.), *Rediscovering Korean Cinema* (Ann Arbor: University of Michigan Press, 2019), pp. 147–59.

Bordwell, David, 'The Idea of Montage in Soviet Art and Film', *Cinema Journal* 11 no. 2 (1972), pp. 9–17.

Bordwell, David, 'You Are My Density,' blog post, davidbordwell.net, 1 November 2011. Available at: <https://www.davidbordwell.net/blog/2011/11/01/you-are-my-density/> (accessed 17 November 2024).

Chang, Kyung-sup, 'Compressed Modernity and its Discontents: South Korean Society in Transition', *Economy and Society* 28 no. 1 (1999), pp. 30–55.

Chang, Kyung-sup, 'Compressed Modernity in South Korea: Constitutive Dimensions, Manifesting Units, and Historical Conditions', in Youna Kim (ed.), *Routledge Handbook of Korean Culture and Society* (New York: Routledge, 2016), pp. 31–47.

Cho, Junhyoung, 'An Early Liberation Zone? The Emergence and Dissolution of the National Motion Picture Ethics Committee' ['*Ttae Irŭn Haebang-gu? Yŏnghwayullijŏn'gugwiwŏnhoeŭi Tŭngjanggwa Haech'e*'], *Webzine*, Research Institute of Korean Studies, 19 August 2014. Available at: <http://rikszine.korea.ac.kr/front/article/humanList.minyeon?selectArticle_id=505&selectCategory_id=61> (accessed 23 November 2022).

Choe, Steve, 'Kim Ki-young's Housemaid Films', in Chung-kang Kim (ed.), *The Films of Kim Ki-young* (Edinburgh: Edinburgh University Press, 2023), pp. 91–106.

Chun, Soonok, *They Are Not Machines: Korean Women Workers and Their Fight for Democratic Trade Unionism in the 1970s* (London: Routledge, 2003).

Chung, Hye Seung, 'Fending Off Darkness, Uplifting National Cinema: Korean Film Censorship and The Stray Bullet', *Situations* 16 no. 1 (31 March 2023), pp. 1–28.

Colomina, Beatriz, *Privacy and Publicity: Modern Architecture as Mass Media* (Cambridge, MA: MIT Press, 1994).

Cumings, Bruce, *Korea's Place in the Sun: A Modern History* (New York: W. W. Norton, 1998).

Eisenstein, Sergei, 'Word and Image', in Eisenstein, *Film Sense*, ed. and trans. Jay Leyda (New York: Harcourt Brace & Company, 1947).

Friedberg, Anne, *The Virtual Window: From Alberti to Microsoft* (Cambridge, MA: MIT Press, 2009).

Frodon, Jean-Michel, '*Hanyŏ the Housemaid*, Kim Ki-young, 1960', in Steven Jay Schneider (ed.), *1001 Movies You Must See Before You Die* (Denver, CO: Peterson's Publishing), p. 373.

Haraway, Donna, 'Situated Knowledges: The Science Question in Feminism and the Privilege of Partial Perspective', *Feminist Studies* 14 no. 3 (Autumn 1988), pp. 575–99.

Hong, Jin-hyuk, 'The Housemaid's Expressionist Mise-en-scène and Modernism – A Style Analysis of Vertical Lines' ['*Hanyŏŭi p'yohyŏnjuŭi mijangsen'gwa modŏnijŭm—sujiksŏnŭl chungshimŭro han sŭt'ail punsŏk*'], *The Korean Journal of Arts Studies* [*Hanguk yesul yŏn'gu*] no. 16 (2017), pp. 239–64.

Kim, Han Sang, '"My" Sweet Home in the Next Decade: The Popular Imagination of Private Homeownership during the Yusin Period', in Youngju Ryu (ed.), *Cultures of Yusin: South Korea in the 1970s* (Ann Arbor: University of Michigan Press, 2018), pp. 119–40.

Kim, Hong-joon (ed.), *Kim Ki-young*, trans. Jung Ye-wŏn (Seoul: Korean Film Council, 2006).

Kim, Ho-yŏng, 'Pre-modernity in Modernity: A Study of Space in Kim Ki-young's Films' ['*Kim Kiyŏng yŏnghwaŭi konggan kujoe nat'ananŭn kŭndaewa chŏn'gŭndaeŭi kaltŭngyangsang*'], *Semiotic Inquiry* [*Gihohak yŏn'gu*] 20 (December 2006), pp. 199–229.

Kim, Ki-young, 'Chu Jŭng-nyŏ's Performance and Life' ['*Kamdogi pon chujungnyŏ: chujungnyŏŭi yŏn'giwa sasaenghwal: chŏnahan pumwigiŭi yŏn'gi – yŏnghwa hanyŏrŭl chungsimŭro*'], *Kukje Yŏnghwa* [International Film] (August 1960), pp. 122–3.

Kim, Ki-young, 'A Film Director's Star Theory' ['*Yŏnghwa kamdogŭi sŭt'aron*'], *The Monthly Cinema* [*Wolgan Yŏnghwa*] (December 1984), pp. 36–7.

Kim, Kyung Hyun, 'Lethal Work: Domestic Space and Gender Troubles in Happy End and The Housemaid', in Kim, *The Remasculinization of Korean Cinema* (Durham, NC, and London: Duke University Press, 2004), pp. 233–58.

Kim, Soyoung, '"Cine-mania"" or Cinephilia: Film Festivals and the Identity Question', in Chi-Yun Shin and Julian Stringer (eds), *New Korean Cinema* (Edinburgh: Edinburgh University Press, 2005). Reprinted from *UTS Review* (now *Cultural Studies Review*) 4 no. 2 (1998), pp. 174–87.

Kim, Soyoung, 'Questions of Woman's Film', in Kathleen McHugh and Nancy Abelmann (eds), *South Korean*

Golden Age Melodrama (Detroit, MI: Wayne State University Press, 2005), pp. 185–200.

Kim, Ye-Rim, 'The Cultural Politics of Developmental Nationalism and Middle-Class Home Fantasy in the Late 1960s' ['*1960nyŏndae chunghuban kaebal naesyŏnŏllijŭmgwa chungsanch'ŭng kajŏng p'ant'ajiŭi munhwajŏngch'i hak*'], *Journal of Korean Modern Literature* [*Hyŏndae munhakŭi yŏn'gu*] 32 (2006), pp. 339–75.

Koo, Hagen, 'Rethinking Korea's Middle Class' ['*Han'gugŭi chungsanch'ŭngŭl tashi saenggak'anda*'], *The Quarterly Changbi (Creation and Criticism)* [*Ch'angjakkwabip'yŏng*] 40 no. 1 (2012), pp. 403–21.

Kwŏn, Podŭrae and Ch'ŏn Chŏnghwan, *To Question the 1960s* [*1960-yŏn ŭl mutta: Pak Chŏng-hŭi sidae ŭi munhwa chŏngch'i wa chisŏng*] (Seoul: Ch'ŏnnyŏn ŭi Sangsang, 2012).

Lee, Hyangjin, 'Family, Death and the *Wonhon* in Four Films of the 1960s', in Alison Peirse and Daniel Martin (eds), *Korean Horror Cinema* (Edinburgh: Edinburgh University Press, 2013), pp. 23–34.

Lee, Nikki J. Y. and Julian Stringer, 'Remake, Repeat, Revive: Kim Ki-young's Housemaid Trilogies', in Claire Perkins and Constantine Verevis (eds), *Film Trilogies: New Critical Approaches* (Basingstoke and New York: Palgrave Macmillan, 2012), pp. 145–63.

Min, Eungjun, Joo Jinsook and Kwak Han Ju, *Korean Film: History, Resistance, and Democratic Imagination* (Westport, CT: Praeger, 2003).

Mok, Hae-jung, 'A Comparative Analysis of Sound in Kim Ki-young's *The Housemaid* and Im Sang-soo's *The Housemaid*' ['*Kim Kiyŏng Hanyŏwa Im Sangsu Hanyŏŭi saundŭ pigyo punsŏk*'], *CineForum* [*Ssinep'orŏm*] no. 11 (2010), pp. 61–96.

Mun, Kŭn-chong, 'A Study on Images of Apartment Housing in Korean Films in the 1930s–60s' ['*1930–60 nyŏndae han'guk yŏnghwae nat'ananŭn ap'at'ŭ imiji yŏn'gu*'], *Journal of the Architectural Institute of Korea* [*Taehan'gŏnch'uk'ak'oe nonmunjip*] (January 2013), pp. 147–58.

Oh, John Kie-chiang, *Korean Politics: The Quest for Democratization and Economic Development* (Ithaca, NY: Cornell University Press, 2018).

Oh, Se-Mi, 'The Cat's Cradle: Middle-Class Optics of Desire in Kim Ki-young's The Housemaid', in Juhn Young Ahn (ed.), *Transgression Korea: Beyond Resistance and Control* (Ann Arbor: University of Michigan Press, 2018), pp. 123–38.

Olenina, Ana Hedberg, *Psychomotor Aesthetics: Movement and Affect in Modern Literature and Film* (Oxford: Oxford University Press, 2020).

Pak, U-sŏng, 'The Performativity and Position of Rats in *The Housemaid*' ['*Hanyŏ esŏ chwiranŭn changch'iga suhaenghanŭn yŏk'algwa wisang – Kim Kiyŏng shinhwaŭi pip'anjŏg chaegorŭl wihan ilgoch'al*'], *Film Studies* [*Yŏnghwa yŏn'gu*] 49 (September 2011), pp. 69–76.

Pak, Yŏng-min, 'Film Study: *Hanyŏ*' ['*Chakp'um yŏn'gu: 'Hanyŏ*'], *Kukje Yŏnghwa* [International Film]

(1961; March issue, published 1 February), pp. 67–9.

Peirse, Alison and Daniel Martin (eds), *Korean Horror Cinema* (Edinburgh: Edinburgh University Press, 2013).

Shin, Arita, 'The Growth of the Korean Middle Class and its Social Consciousness', *The Developing Economies* XLI no. 2 (June 2003), pp. 201–20.

Shin Jŏngch'ŏl, '[Conversations with Directors] Kim Ki-young, Veteran Director Pursuing a New World in Works' ['*Yŏnghwagamdokkwaŭi taedam] Kim Kiyŏng, saeroun chakp'umsegyerŭl ch'uguhanŭn nojang kamdok*'], *The Monthly Cinema* [*Wŏlgan Yŏnghwa*] (October 1984), pp. 52–5.

Sobchack, Vivian, 'Afterword: Media Archaeology and Re-presencing the Past', in Erkki Huhtamo and Jussi Parikka (eds), *Media Archaeology: Approaches, Applications, and Implications* (Los Angeles: University of California Press, 2011), pp. 323–33.

Suhr, Christian and Rane Willerslev, 'Introduction: Montage as an Amplifier of Invisibility', in Suhr and Willerslev (eds), *Transcultural Montage* (New York: Berghahn Books, 2013), pp. 1–16.

Vidler, Anthony, 'The Explosion of Space: Architecture and the Filmic Imaginary', *Assemblage* no. 21 (August 1993), pp. 45–59.

Yi, Ch'ŏl-chae, 'A Study on Characteristics of Interior Space in Korean Classic Films – Space in 1960s Homes as Seen in the Expressionist Film *Hanyŏ*' ['*Han'guk kojŏnyŏnghwarŭl t'onghae pon shillae konggan t'ŭksŏnge kwanhan yŏn'gu—p'yohyŏnjuŭi yŏnghwa hanyŏe nat'anan 1960nyŏndae chut'aekkongganŭl chungshimŭro*'], *Korean Institute of Interior Design Journal* [*Hanguksillaedijainhak'oe nonmunjip*] 21 no. 2 (April 2012), pp. 65–73.

Yi, Dae-bŏm and Chŏng Su-wan, '"Outsiders", the Symbol of Compressed Modernization in the Housemaid Trilogy' ['*Hanyŏyŏnjage nat'anan apch'ukchŏg kŭndaehwaŭi tamjich'erosŏ oebuin*'] *CineForum* [*Ssinep'orŏm*] no. 28 (2017), pp. 37–73.

Yi, Hyo-in, *Thirteen Korean Film Directors* [*Hangukŭi yŏnghwa gamdok 13-in*] (Paju: Yŏllinch'aektŭl, 1994).

Yi, Hyo-in, 'Biography', in Kim Hong-joon (ed.), *Kim Ki-young*, trans. Jung Ye-wŏn (Seoul: Korean Film Council, 2006).

Yi, Yŏn-ho, 'Director Kim Ki-young: Half a Century of Solitude and Love of Thirty-one Films' ['*Kim Kiyŏng gamdok banbaeknyŏnŭi godokkwa sŏrŭn hanaŭi yŏnghwa sarang*'], *KINO* (January 1997), pp. 38–45.

Yi, Yŏn-ho, *Hanyo* DVD booklet, *Re-birth of the Classics: Hanyo* (Korean Film Archive Collection, 2009).

Yu, Ji-hyŏng (ed.), *24 Years of Conversation: Interviews with Director Kim Ki-young* [*Isipsanyŏngan ŭi daehwa: Kim Ki-young gamdok intŏbyujip*] (Seoul: Sun, 2006).